TO LOOK
CLOSELY

TO LOOK CLOSELY

CLOSELY

SCIENCE AND LITERACY IN THE NATURAL WORLD

LAURIE RUBIN

STENHOUSE PUBLISHERS
PORTLAND, MAINE

Stenhouse Publishers
www.stenhouse.com

Credits
"To Look at Any Thing" from *The Living Seed* by John Moffitt. Copyright © 1961 by John Moffitt, renewed 1989 by Henry Moffitt. Reprinted by permission of Houghton Mifflin Harcourt Publishing Company. All rights reserved.

Photo Credits
Figures 4.9, 4.10, 5.8, 5.10, and back cover photo (journals on a log) by Elizabeth Bunting
Author photo by Jo-Marcia Todd
All other photos by Laurie Rubin

Library of Congress Cataloging-in-Publication Data
Rubin, Laurie, 1947-
  To look closely : science and literacy in the natural world / Laurie Rubin.
     pages cm
  Includes bibliographical references.
  ISBN 978-1-57110-992-7 (pbk. : alk. paper) -- ISBN 978-1-62531-001-9 (ebook) 1. Science-
-Study and teaching (Elementary) 2. Nature--Study and teaching (Elementary) 3. Language
arts--Correlation with content subjects. I. Title.
  LB1585.R84 2013
  372.35'044--dc23
                          2013021969

Cover and interior design by Blue Design, Portland, Maine (bluedes.com)

Manufactured in the United States of America

PRINTED ON 30% PCW
RECYCLED PAPER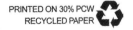

19 18 17 16 15 14 13   9 8 7 6 5 4 3 2 1

For Lauren and Katherine

For all my students, past, present, and future

CONTENTS

Acknowledgments

I always read acknowledgments. As a matter of fact, I read them first, turning to those pages before starting the book in my hand. As a reader, I want to get acquainted with the author through the colleagues, friends, and family members being thanked. As an aspiring writer, I looked for clues about the writing process and about the people who might help me become a published author one day. That day, as it turns out, has been over twenty years in the making, and now it is my turn to acknowledge the teachers, students, and friends who helped me embrace the writing life and connect to the natural world.

Having entered the teaching profession later than most, I was fortunate to work with a group of experienced, reflective colleagues who informed and inspired my own teaching. In particular, I owe thanks to four passionate mentors: Jo Todd for introducing me to walks outside and monarch caterpillars right from the start; Kathy McLaren for sharing her models of consensus decision making and integrated curriculum; Ann Caren for creating a venue to reflect on teaching practice and suggesting that we ask students, What are you thinking? and Ann Halpern for teaching me to value children's play, know my students' interests, and honor their choices.

I first attended the Literacy Institutes at the University of New Hampshire to find out whether I was a writer, and if so, what I was supposed to write about. I consider the eight summers I continued to spend in Durham to be a turning point in my teaching career. As I learned new strategies for teaching reading and writing to my students, new ways of thinking about my own literacy became critical to my ongoing growth and energy as a teacher and as a writer. Thank you to Louise Wrobleski for thought-provoking classes on the reading/writing connection and for providing a venue to go public with my writing for the first time. To Maureen Barbieri for the Moffitt poem, for deepening my love of poetry, and for nurturing efforts to write my own. To Meredith Hall for seeing me as a writer first, thus significantly raising the bar for my writing craft. To Kate Gardoqui for leading me back to the natural world with wisdom and joy and for helping me through my first book proposal.

I also recognize the educators and researchers who became my teachers through their books and upon whose ideas I built and finessed my own curricula—Lucy Calkins, Ralph Fletcher, Donald Graves, Georgia Heard, Ellin Keene, Donald Murray, and Katie Wood Ray.

My appreciation runs deep for the students who inspired me and confirmed my belief that a connection to nature was the most vital part of our education together. Although some names have been changed to protect their privacy, it is my students and their love of the natural world, the experiences we shared together, and the subsequent dialogue from the classroom that brings authenticity to the text. I also thank all the parents who valued nature study, the families who saved their children's nature journals so that I could share the entries in this book, and the many visiting experts (both community members and parents) who volunteered their time to share their knowledge of the natural world with my students and me.

Closer to home, I owe thanks to my partner, David Ruth, for moments of science, invigorating conversations about teaching practice, and showing me how to see the world as a scientist. To my daughter, Sarah Moore, for *Ego Sum Scriptoris*—believing in me as a writer—and for speedy, intelligent editing at a moment's notice, thank you. Thanks to Sebastian Ruth for suggesting I use a digital recorder to chronicle all the nature-based happenings at the end of the school day, which ultimately became the vignettes in this book.

I am so fortunate to have arrived at the door of Stenhouse Publishers where the entire team is supportive, considerate, and was always willing to answer my many questions along the way—Jill Cooley, Chris Downey, Jay Kilburn, and Philippa Stratton.

Heartfelt gratitude to my editor Maureen Barbieri, who guided me through the proposal, revision, and delivery of this book with insight, incredibly respectful feedback, tremendous warmth, and love. I could not have asked for a more generous, compassionate, and affirming experience.

In the end, it is my readers who made it all happen. Thank you to Richard Nowagrodski for astute line editing and never failing to ask, "How's the book going?"; to Betsy Kolasky for the ongoing conversation, for smart revision ideas, and for believing I was the best possible person to write this book; and to Wendy Wallitt, my writing buddy, whose companionship I treasured and judgment I trusted, who was there from the very first vignette and without whom this book would not exist.

To Look at Any Thing

To look at any thing,
If you would know that thing,
You must look at it long:
To look at this green and say
"I have seen spring in these
Woods," will not do—you must
Be the thing you see:
You must be the dark snakes of
Stems and ferny plumes of leaves,
You must enter in
To the small silences between
The leaves,
You must take your time
And touch the very peace
They issue from.

—JOHN MOFFITT

Why Nature Study?

For many years, during the last two weeks in August, you would find me setting up my classroom—organizing areas for books, art supplies, and blocks; making labels for cubbies and coat hooks; writing an introductory letter to parents; reviewing first-week plans; and attending to a seemingly endless to-do list. Then, on Labor Day weekend, you would find me searching through fields and roadsides, turning over telltale, chewed-up milkweed leaves, hoping to stumble on a fat green monarch caterpillar beneath. This ritual hunt launched my very first year of teaching when my mentor and first-grade colleague informed me that I had to start the school year with monarch caterpillars in my room. It was the best piece of advice she ever gave me. I learned early on that children and the natural world are a winning combination.

Year after year my students and I marveled as each J-shaped caterpillar miraculously morphed into its chrysalis and then, two weeks later, the same green gem turned clear and hatched an orange and black monarch butterfly. I was always on the lookout for new patches of milkweed to enhance my autumnal supply of caterpillars. Then, unexpectedly, there came a year with no monarchs, and I panicked. How could I coax my new crop of second graders into a community of engaged, curious learners without my beloved caterpillars?

With only seven days before school would begin, I sat down in my classroom, my planning book open in front of me, staring out the window and waiting for inspiration. I considered the tanks filled with turtles and frogs, a permanent installation in the classroom across the hall. I remembered the aquarium a colleague set up the previous year to study water flow. I stepped out into the small woods just twenty feet from my classroom window and stood in front of the shale streambed at the edge of the school property where a small trickle of water was flowing. That night I scoured my professional collection of books on science education and hit the jackpot—an essay about a yearlong stream study. I could feel the adrenalin rush as I decided to give stream study a try, hoping to find a scientist/ecologist or two among my students' parents to help me. With nothing more than a general idea that my students would observe changes in the stream as well as the plant and animal life surrounding it, I reasoned that as long as I could engage my students in the natural world, I would figure out the details later. I trusted that my students' engagement, curiosity, wonder, and connection to nature would show me the way and inform my teaching.

For the next two years I experimented with different approaches, trying to identify the important concepts I wanted to teach via nature and outdoor exploration. I knew there was a lot of fine-tuning ahead of me, but, in the meantime, I was learning a great deal about aquatic insects, geology, and environmental issues from volunteer parents, and I was encouraged by the enthusiasm of my students. It turned out some of them were already seasoned naturalists, adept at catching salamanders and crayfish, knowing exactly where to find them.

In retrospect, it is a logical progression that in July 2004 I enroll in a nature journaling class at the University of New Hampshire in Durham, my fourth summer attending the Literacy Institutes for teachers. This particular year I drive the seven-plus hours from Ithaca to Durham chuckling over the prospect of earning graduate credit to wander about outdoors, drawing and writing observations in a blank book. I am not sure how this class will inform my teaching, but I look forward to using my brand-new set of Prismacolor pencils and improving my drawing skills.

Kate Gardoqui, our talented and passionate instructor, has already sent us the syllabus. As soon I arrive, I begin scoping out my "sit spot." We are to visit this place every day to observe and connect with the natural world. By the first day of class, with convenience in mind, I choose a small stream just off the path that I will walk several times a day. By the end of the first day, I am hooked.

Over the next two weeks, I immerse myself in nature study. I learn that animals stay near the edges when they are eating so they can quickly elude a predator. I observe a water strider long enough to discover that it moves by stroking with its middle legs and I recognize that there are more flowers on the *southern* side of a goldenrain tree. I return to my sit spot a dozen times until I feel like I am returning to visit an old friend. Somewhere in the middle of choosing a final class project, I grasp the obvious. I will add nature journaling to our stream study.

Shortly after my return from UNH, I am vacationing in the Pacific Northwest where my nature journal becomes my most treasured companion. Every outing, every hike suddenly requires an extra hour or two. On the Naches Trail around Mt. Rainier, I need to write about the two squirrels in residence at a popular lookout, lobbying for lunch scraps. I am compelled to draw the Indian paintbrush so I will always remember it. Back in Seattle, I borrow my friend's field guides and identify the rufous hummingbird I have been watching for an hour in his front yard. I slowly give myself over to a passion for the natural world, a passion that will change my life and the lives of my students.

It is during the next year that I slowly begin to identify myself as a naturalist, meaning for me, a person drawn to the natural world, eager to identify the flora and fauna around her. I fill up three small journals with drawings and observations. I become a birdwatcher who never travels anywhere without her binoculars. I start collecting Mary Oliver's nature poems and write one of my own trying to capture my profound attraction to birds. I memorize John Moffitt's *To Look at Anything* and tape up a copy in my bathroom for all my friends and family members to read. I beam when a student shows me an entry in the nature journal he is keeping at home. I laugh with delight when a parent excitedly points out a downy woodpecker at a class picnic. I become the nature maven in my school, receiving gifts of bones, feathers, and "sightings" from students and teachers alike. I am convinced that encouraging my students to observe and connect to the natural world is the most valuable set of lifelong lessons I can deliver.

Over time nature study becomes the heart and soul of my teaching. Over time nature study not only helps me create an integrated curriculum throughout the day but also informs and enhances my students' learning in science, math, and language arts. Over time nature study teaches my students and me how to be critical thinkers.

❋ ❋ ❋

When I started teaching in 1987 the whole language movement was in full swing. It was an exciting time and a great fit for me. My personal language arts skills made a giant leap when I began to teach reading and writing. Writing for real purposes and mimicking the process of published authors jump-started my own writing. The emphasis on reading for meaning, and later on metacognition, changed the way I read books and transformed the discussions in my book club.

Although I was excited and thrilled to enter the teaching profession in the midst of such a reflective examination of language arts teaching practice, not all teachers felt the same way. It did not take long for seasoned teachers, those teaching for twenty years or more, to shake their heads knowingly and proclaim, "What goes around, comes around. Wait a few years and we'll be back to where we were in the early seventies." I remember a fourth-grade teacher stopping by my classroom to confide, "Just wait. In ten years the pendulum will swing back again. One hundred eighty." I listened with the confused, overwhelmed, but also partly arrogant ears of a first-year teacher and opted for the meaningful whole language text of the New Zealand readers over the Modern Curriculum phonics-based readers with contrived sentences like "The cat and the rat sat on the mat."

It was also a time when my colleagues and mentors valued integrated learning. In our school it was common for teachers to teach by theme. For example, over the course of one year my first-grade class investigated Families, Simple Machines, Thailand, and Water Animals. Our learning in all content areas—math, language arts, science, and social studies—revolved around one of these central themes. Even the music, art, gym, and library teachers were willing to explore ways to incorporate our themes into their required curricula.

Then, as predicted by my more senior colleagues, in 2001 the passage of the No Child Left Behind Act did, in fact, begin the trajectory back toward an emphasis on teaching isolated skills. With the best of intentions, Republicans and Democrats came together to pass legislation they believed would improve individual outcomes in education by setting high standards and establishing measurable goals. However, despite pressures from the No Child Left Behind Act, and with many of my colleagues returning to skills-based teaching, I believed that an integrated learning experience could actually take children beyond the minimum skill levels needed for standardized tests.

Today my belief in an integrated learning experience for my students remains resolute. I am confident that such an experience can be developed within the context of the ever-shifting state and federal learning standards. I am convinced that nature study is *the* child-centered program that can integrate critical thinking skills in science, mathematics, and language arts.

If you are a preservice or inservice teacher reading this book, I hope to convince you to place nature study at the core of your curriculum, even if you, like me, might not identify yourself at first as a scientist or scientific thinker. If you are a school administrator, I hope to persuade you to walk around your school and envision students engaged in an outdoor curriculum that leads to critical thinking and future stewardship of our environment. If you are a parent or grandparent, I hope you will be inspired to go out into the natural world with your children and grandchildren, find a sit spot, and create memories together that will last a lifetime.

❋   ❋   ❋

To Look Closely: Science and Literacy in the Natural World documents my experience with nature study and the development of my curriculum. It follows my class of second graders from September through June as they visit a woodland stream.

Chapter 1, "Ten Tips for Getting Started on Nature Study," outlines the nuts and bolts necessary to plan for a year of nature study. You will not only find out about the practical considerations of time, management, equipment, and supervision, but also consider how to boost your comfort level in the out-of-doors and prepare your students to be naturalists.

Chapter 2, "Moments of Science," demonstrates how recognizing moments of science sets a tone of inquiry-based thinking in the classroom for every content area, throughout the day and throughout the school year. When you use moments of science as a convention in your teaching, you will understand, from

FIGURE 1 - A student remembers a friend he made in the natural world.

a Salamander
Friend...

Me and gregory
were great freind.
Until I'ley him
go. I made him
A little of natural
house for him.
I still have great
memorys.

the inside out, what it means to have an inquiry-based science curriculum. As you learn to notice moments of science, your students will start responding to the world around them in increasingly perceptive ways and thinking together as a community of scientists. You will understand the different kinds of student moments, how you can introduce and integrate moments of science into your teaching practice, and how to encourage critical thinking skills at home.

Chapters 3, 4, and 5, "A Year at the Stream—Autumn, Winter, Spring," describe a year of nature study in upstate New York and show what it looks and sounds like when a class of twenty-one second graders visits a small stream in the woods behind a suburban elementary school. Following each of the thirteen stream visits, you will find my reflections about our class discussions, activities, and learning experiences. As you read, I hope you will ponder my observations made over time about group dynamics and individual students. My personal nature journal entries will show you my attempts to practice the critical thinking I am asking of my students. Finally, you will read samples of student journal entries, collected over seven years of nature study, which show a variety of student abilities (see Figure 1).

Chapter 6, "Literacy Through Nature Study—Reading," demonstrates how the natural world provides our students with multiple opportunities to develop the language of metacognition. As children become naturalists, as they strive to understand the world they live in, as they learn to observe, ask questions, make hypotheses, and look for evidence in the natural world, they are also rehearsing essential reading comprehension strategies that will enhance their literary lives. You will learn how to use experiences in the natural world to teach your students how to make connections and inferences, ask questions, visualize, and determine importance when they read. You will appreciate how critical thinking skills extend from moments of science to moments of language that celebrate questions and observations about words, text, and writing craft.

Chapter 7, "Literacy Through Nature Study—Writing," considers how nature study motivates a variety of writing genres. You will discover how shared experiences in the natural world inspire students to write throughout the school year. Stream visits and bird study coupled with student sharing of rocks, feathers, bones, and creatures in the classroom maintain a focus toward nature and the environment, providing a ready-made treasure chest of writing topics. You will examine student work in narrative, poetic, and nonnarrative genres, including nature journals.

Chapter 8, "Creating Stewards of the Natural World," illustrates how a focus on nature study nurtures "green" citizens who grow up to value and protect the natural environment. You will meet students who refine their understanding of the natural world inside the classroom and at home, who pursue a particular inquiry over time, and who are inspired by the opportunity for environmental activism.

In the appendixes, you will find examples of student writing—narrative and poetry—that represent a range of ability. There is also a list of nature-based websites for students to use independently, for teachers to gain background knowledge, or for whole-class instruction. The references offer a quick guide to the picture books that I use for read-alouds in my classroom.

After joining us at the stream and listening in to our conversations in the classroom, I hope you will agree with me that nature study is not an enrichment activity, but instead the essential key to fostering creative, inquiry-based learning throughout the year, extended to all curricular areas. I hope you will have many students like the ones you meet in this book—Sophie, Samantha, Nicholas, Jocelyn, Daniel, and Sydney, to name a few—to inspire and encourage you to look outside and embrace a year of nature study.

CHAPTER 1

Ten Tips for Getting Started on Nature Study

As elementary school teachers we know the power of modeling for our students. We usually spend the first month of school training them to respect each other and the classroom materials and to internalize the routines and responsibilities that will support a creative and productive learning environment throughout the year. I schedule regular practice for my second-grade students to pass a morning greeting as they sit in a circle on the rug, line up to leave the room, return blocks to the proper shelf, and take turns in a math game. I model how to choose an appropriate book to read, how to brainstorm topics for writing a story, where to write "name and date" on a sheet of paper, how to use the glue or masking tape without waste, and on and on.

Before I introduce something for the first time, I try it out myself at home or after school to discover surprises or unexpected difficulties. Then, in front of my students, I write a story, think aloud about a book I am reading, or demonstrate how to show my thinking for a math problem on paper. My students not only learn the procedure but also pay closer attention when they can sneak a peek into the personal life of their teacher. I apply these same teaching strategies to nature study.

TIP #1. BECOME A NATURALIST YOURSELF

If you have not yet made time in your life to linger in the natural world, this is the moment to start. As you begin to make your own discoveries, ask your own questions, and meet your own friends in the natural world, you will be learning how to guide your students to do the same. You will find yourself checking out field guides from the library to identify the unknown plants or animals you encounter. And you will accumulate your own stories to tell.

The first step is to choose your own sit spot, a "secret" spot near your school or your home. Pick at least one day a week to visit and just sit. Take in what is around you. Bring a journal with you and, if you feel like it, write or draw. Go at different times of the day if you can. See what happens. (The sit spot is a core routine of the Kamana Naturalist Training Program. The idea was first developed by Tom Brown Jr. in his courses at the Tracker School and was further developed by Jon Young and instructors at the Wilderness Awareness School in Duvall, Washington. Check out their website at http://wildernessawareness.org/kamana/.)

I go to my sit spot once a week, a section of Six Mile Creek in Ithaca, a small university city in upstate New York, home to Cornell University and Ithaca College. I marvel that although it is only one block from the house I have lived in for fifteen years, until recently I had never visited this spot before.

It is quiet and peaceful here, and if I stay long enough, I forget that I am in a city. When I close my eyes, I can hear the water flowing by and I feel transported to the country home where I used to live. One day I get lost counting how many mallards go swimming by and wonder if I am count-ing the same birds more than once. Another evening I discover slug trails along the concrete wall, glistening under the streetlight. I make many new friends—spiders, insects, trees, animals. I have learned to expect the unex-pected: in a million years, I never imagined I would meet a great blue heron in my urban neighborhood. These experiences become the stories and the nature journal entries that I share with my students before we begin our stream study. For example:

September 14, 2004, 9:20 p.m.

As I approach the creek, the first thing that I see—highlighted in the lamp-light—is a great blue heron! The blue seems to sense my presence because as I walk closer, down the bank, it also walks farther down the creek into the darkness. It stops when I stop. Every once in a while it stretches out its long elegant neck but otherwise stays planted, not at all perturbed by two neighborhood dogs that soon come by. When I leave fifteen minutes later, it is still there.

Does the heron come here every night? What was it doing? Does it sleep standing in the water? Where does it winter? Does it have a mate?

As I turn to leave, filled with emotion about this newfound peaceful connection to nature that has entered my life, I see what looks like a sparkly rhinestone necklace outlined on the cement wall. Thinking it may be a spider's web I walk closer. Right in the middle of the wall are two two-inch slugs curled around each other. I am looking at their trails, made glittery in the light of the street lamps. I am filled with gratitude that I can discover so much at night.

TIP #2. FIT NATURE STUDY INTO YOUR WEEKLY SCHEDULE

When I read books on teaching reading, writing, or mathematics, at some point I start squirming in my seat. I want to scream at the authors. If I adopt their practices (and there are so many good ones out there), I know I will be preparing, teaching, and assessing for one content area three to four hours a day. Don't they know I have other subjects to teach?

In addition to the basic three, I also teach social studies, science, health, personal safety, and computer literacy. This year my students study Spanish for an hour a week. Community organizations—constantly on the prowl for warm second-grade bodies—offer curricula on Halloween safety, fire safety, sun safety, composting, recycling, nutrition, pet care, and more. Why do I fit in nature study?

I fit in nature study because I am extremely motivated to do so. The more I take my students out into the natural world, the more we discover together, the more we look forward to our next outdoor adventure, the more I know I have landed on something special. Then in June a former student slips into

FIGURE 1.1 - A bulletin board portraying the joy and wonder of the natural world greets students as they enter the classroom.

my classroom once a week to leave a perfectly flattened out gingko leaf on my desk as a gift. Over the summer I hear that a kindergarten parent is already hoping her child will be in my class because I "take them outside in all kinds of weather." Affirmations like these inspire me to find ways to integrate nature study throughout the day, throughout the year. And I make sure my students know how much I value this study by strategically locating a bulletin board right above their cubbies (the first place they go every morning) entitled Making Friends in the Natural World. Color photographs clipped out of magazines compete for space with gifts of student artwork that I rotate regularly (see Figure 1.1).

When I get my "specials" schedule in the fall (music, gym, art, and library), the first thing I do is pencil in one afternoon a week for nature study and science. The exact day will be determined by the availability of volunteers, but I steer away from Mondays or Fridays. Not only do we miss many Mondays and Fridays for school holidays, but I also need time for opening and closing routines on those days.

I devote four afternoons of the week primarily to teaching mathematics. On the fifth day we will benefit from the intersection of scientific and mathematical concepts. Nature study not only incorporates essential second-grade mathematical content but also provides the opportunity to practice skills for authentic purposes. Measurement (linear, temperature, speed), data collection and analysis (line and bar graphs), estimation, and prediction are regular components of our outdoor inquiry.

When I take my students out into the natural world, I want them to have enough time to explore, respond to a particular focus I have planned, write and draw in their nature journals, and participate in a follow-up discussion/sharing session with the whole class. We need at least an hour; two is even better, and if it were up to my students, they would want even more time for exploring. Usually we land somewhere in the middle at an hour and a half.

In September and October we go to our stream site once a week. By November, the likelihood of more inclement weather and the additional time needed to integrate other second-grade science curricula combine to reduce stream study to monthly visits. When we are not outside at the stream, we move our nature study indoors. In November, I set up a bird feeder outside our classroom window to launch a yearlong bird study and I also turn my attention to the FOSS science kits I am required to use—Air and Weather and Insects.

When I read the manuals for the first time, I look for connections between nature study and the concepts introduced in the kits. I am more interested in how the FOSS curricula will enrich our experience in the natural world, rather than how nature study will fit in with the kits. I choose to teach Air and Weather in the fall because this module prepares us for examining seasonal weather changes at the stream all year. I teach Insects in the spring because the insects we observe in the classroom inform our discovery of insect eggs, larvae, pupae, and adults at the stream as the days warm.

Once you get started on nature study, you will not be able to stop. The magic of the natural world will show up in your students' stories and poems (see Chapter 7). Parents will tell you about their children's explorations at home.

The engagement and excitement of your students will energize you. You too will find the time to teach nature study.

TIP #3. PICK A SECRET SIT SPOT FOR THE CLASS TO VISIT THROUGHOUT THE YEAR

Try to find a little piece of the natural world that is close to your school. Depending on your school's rural, urban, or suburban community, it could be a stream, pond, woods, beach, hillside, desert, marsh, orchard, park, hedgerow, grassy lot, or field. And don't overlook a single tree visible from your classroom window, a patch of grass, a row of shrubs or bushes, cracks in the sidewalk, or a drainage ditch. Of course, the larger the area, the more your class can spread out with enough space for each student to make independent discoveries. Ideally your sit spot should be accessible all year long because you want your students to have the opportunity to observe nature closely as it changes through the seasons.

We have a small wood behind our school—primarily maple, oak, wild cherry, white pine, and pignut hickory. There is a small creek bed at the edge of the school property, which is usually bone dry when we start the school year. Rather than give my whole class access to the entire stream, I create three small groups of six to eight students, depending on the size of my class.

Each group is assigned to a section of the stream about six to eight meters long with several meters of buffer space in between. The stream is the class "secret" sit spot, but each stream section becomes home to a different group. Each year when we first start stream study, I name the groups Red, Green, and Blue, identified by colored pieces of yarn wrapped around the tree trunks to mark each section. After a month of visits to the stream, I invite each group to choose its own "natural" name—a plant, animal, habitat, or phenomenon. For the most part, groups explore their own sit spots and save their finds for our culminating group share on the lawn adjacent to the school in the fall and spring, or back in the classroom on cold winter days. But from time to time, two adjacent groups will come together to share a particularly exciting discovery (usually a crayfish or salamander) that just cannot wait.

On the morning of our first stream study, we make a circle on the rug and I tell my students about my own secret sit spot. I make it clear that a secret spot is secret not because it is hidden from view but because it is special to the person who has chosen it. I also clarify that young children might need to ask parents for permission when choosing an outdoor sit spot.

Next I invite students to tell us where their secret spots are located. Invariably with no hesitation, almost everyone shares a secret spot; some have two or three. The students who pass at first (always an option when we go around the circle making comments), unsure about what exactly qualifies as a secret spot, are eager to share after they hear examples from their classmates. They start with outdoor spots—trees, fields, woods, streams, and bushes. Indoor spots are "on my bed," "behind the couch," or "in a closet." There is a special feeling in the classroom—secret spots are private but full of adventure. The sparkle in their eyes, the excitement in their voices is palpable in the room. My students are ready to make their own friends in the natural world.

TIP #4. ADDRESS SAFETY CONSIDERATIONS

Before you take your class into the natural world, familiarize yourself with any outdoor hazards in your region. In New York State, I need to teach my students about three hazards—poison ivy, deer ticks, and bees and wasps. I believe that, rather than frightening children, the information empowers and gives them a sense of security.

A few days before going out for the first time, we gather on the rug to talk about being safe in the natural world. I quickly present these facts about deer ticks, bees, and wasps: "Deer ticks carry Lyme disease. They hang out near the ground and when you go by, they reach out from their perches on stems and leaves to hook onto your clothing.

"To keep ticks off your body, wear light-colored clothing (long-sleeved shirt and pants.) It is also a good idea to tuck your pants into your socks to prevent a tick from crawling up your leg. If a tick does land on you, the light colors will make it easier to spot. Always do a tick check (ask a grownup to help) after a day in the woods or grassy fields.

"Just like people, bees and wasps do not like to have their homes destroyed. Do not poke a stick into holes in the ground where wasp nests might be hiding. Avoid jumping on brush piles or rotten stumps that could be a home for yellow jackets. If you know you are allergic to bees or wasps, talk to your parents before going outside so you know what to do if you get stung." (When I have students with bee sting allergies, I always follow school procedures and carry a cell phone and their EpiPens outside with me.)

I spend the most time talking about poison ivy since we do have a small patch growing near the stream. I explain that some people are allergic to poison ivy and some are not, so it is a good idea to know what it looks like. I tell them that I am *very* allergic to poison ivy, but I turned fifty-six before I learned to recognize it! They will be much better informed than I was.

"There are general rules to identify poison ivy, but he is always a trickster. Poison ivy usually has sets of three leaflets, but what if one fell off in a storm? The middle leaflet always has a longer stem than the two side leaflets. The main stems are usually not quite straight but they may be on a baby plant. The stems can be woody or not.

"Poison ivy can be green or red, shiny or dull. It can be a bush growing low to the ground, a vine climbing up a tree or just roots without leaves. The leaflets can have different shapes, some can point up and some down. In summer you might see green berries on some plants and in the fall the berries turn white.

"It is the oil from a poison ivy plant that can irritate your skin and make you itch like crazy. If you think you have touched poison ivy, wash your hands as soon as you get home, then jump in the shower and scrub yourself with soap and water to wash off the oil.

"So if you see a plant with three leaflets, look it over carefully. If you're not sure, assume it is poison ivy and stay away. And remember, 'hairy rope, don't be a dope; leaflets three, let it be.'"

Fortunately bees and wasps are only occasional visitors at our stream site, and we have never encountered deer ticks. I always claim the stream section with the poison ivy patch as my own, and I remind my group to walk around it as we approach.

A certain respect for the natural world comes from being aware of its dangers. Just as we try to move quietly in the woods, replace overturned rocks or leaf piles and return all live animals to their habitats, we keep our eyes and ears open for natural hazards and we feel safe.

TIP #5. RECRUIT AND ORGANIZE VOLUNTEERS

During our school's open house, the day before classes begin, I pass out a Parent Volunteer Form listing all the volunteer opportunities in my classroom. At the top of the list I write, "Stream Study/Science—Join us once a week. Two volunteers needed on the same afternoon. It is helpful to have a substitute volunteer for backup as well (12:15–2:00 p.m.). Best days are Tuesday, Wednesday, or Thursday."

Most volunteers in my classroom begin in mid-October, but I try to identify two parents who can make a yearlong commitment to stream study and other science explorations by the second or third week in September. I want to hook my students on the natural world as soon as possible, and it works best to have them in small groups with an adult supervising each group.

So far I have been lucky enough to recruit sufficient volunteers from among my students' families. If that were not possible, I would reach out to the community: nature-oriented organizations, senior citizen centers, college graduate programs, or retired teacher friends.

By the second week of school, I have a sense of my students as learners, enough to create groups that usually work for the rest of the year. Just as it is important to visit the same sit spot over time until it feels like home, it is equally valuable to cultivate a family of naturalists who begin to recognize each other's strengths in the natural world and who develop a history of experiences together. I keep the students who need more behavioral support with me, and usually parents have their own children in their groups. The rest of the students are placed to make balanced groupings much as we create balanced classes to pass on to third grade each year—balanced by gender, academic skills, behavior, and in this case, experience with the natural world.

I ask parents to join us right after recess. They listen to an introductory lesson, a read-aloud, class discussions, or our predictions about what we will encounter at the stream (see Figure 1.2). When I outline the focus and expectations for the day, parents can ask questions and clarify their own roles as group leaders. Despite my best intentions and frequent check-ins, sometimes it will take me weeks to find out that a parent is struggling with a particular student who is *not* being a "good listener." Usually a three-way conversation with parent, student, and teacher will straighten out the difficulty, but on occasion I will move a challenging student to my group for the rest of the year.

For the most part, parents who choose to volunteer for stream study already have an affinity for the natural world. When they also happen to work in environmental sciences, I defer to their expertise on a regular basis. Thanks to the knowledge and keen observation skills of parents, my students and I have been introduced to water pennies, slime mold, and wild geranium.

FIGURE 1.2 - Parent volunteers are an integral part of stream study, arriving in time to hear the day's plan.

TIP #6. USE COMMUNITY RESOURCES

I am a happy and engaged teacher when I am learning right along with my students. Maybe that is why I am always looking for experts to come into my classroom and enrich *our* studies. In a college community there are many opportunities knocking on our door. The most frequent request is from professors who want their undergraduate students to come in and present a final project, often on a particular animal—spiders, insects, frogs, you name it. Undergraduate presentations usually result in my students' staring at a single poster (or more recently, too many PowerPoint slides) and squirming through a thirty-minute mini-lecture. Instead I look for the professors who are willing to come in themselves.

Further, it is the interests and questions from my students that determine which experts I call upon. If we are not studying spiders, I do not invite a spider expert. I want my students to have sufficient background knowledge to be informed and attentive listeners. I want them to have questions on the tips of their tongues or natural objects waiting in their cubbies that they are eager to identify. This is why, each fall, I usually invite a tree expert to visit us.

Getting Ready for the Tree Expert

In mid- to late October the New York landscape is at the height of its fall color. As the trees begin to drop their leaves, my students come back to class after recess laden with colorful gifts. We examine one or two a day and my students are constantly "talking trees." Jose recognizes the maple leaf from the Canadian flag. That reminds Ana of the Japanese maple in her front yard. Chloe knows an acorn comes from an oak tree. Tom, Stella, and Kieran have apple trees in their yards. I decide it must be time to meet the trees that live near our stream.

In preparation for this day, I arrange for a tree expert to help us identify our new friends in the natural world. I access the resources available to me in our town. For a few years, Andy Hillman, the city forester, was able to join us. When he could no longer fit school visits into his busy schedule, Nina Bassuk, a Cornell University professor of urban horticulture, arranged for Barbara Conolly, one of her graduate students, to work with us.

Before Barbara comes to visit, we get ready. The poem of the week is "Autumn" by Kristine O'Connell George, which celebrates trees "setting the hills ablaze" (1998, 39). In *Meeting Trees*, Scott Russell Sanders makes tree identification a joyful game and introduces some of the features to look for—leaves, bark, and seeds. *Crinkleroot's Guide to Knowing the Trees* by Jim Arnosky goes into more detail and prepares us for Barbara's lesson on compound and simple leaves. I also take out tree field guides from the school library to supplement my personal and classroom collections.

On stream study day, I present our task. "Today we will gather leaves at the stream to get ready for our tree expert next week. Please look for leaves on the ground and find as many different kinds as you can, but only bring back one or two of each kind."

When we return to the classroom, I introduce field guides for the first time. I highlight the important features and model the different ways to look up a tree.

"Please go to your tables and use the field guides you find there to see how many leaves you can identify. When you are done, put each leaf inside the pages of the dictionary to press them flat."

Even with parent volunteers facilitating, this is a difficult task. I am not expecting much positive identification to occur. The pages for maples and oaks alone show at least a dozen species each. My students will simply add field guides to their natural-world tool belts, and hopefully they will pay closer attention to Barbara's presentation the following week.

My e-mail exchanges with Barbara review the basics:

1. Second graders can listen well for twenty to thirty minutes.
2. Keep it simple—one or two concepts at most.

The Tree Expert Arrives

On the day Barbara arrives, my students file in after recess and several go right up to her. "Are you the tree expert?" they query. They soon form a circle on the rug and Barbara begins. Within the first few minutes I recognize that the combination of Barbara's bubbly enthusiasm and clear simple language are a perfect fit. She uses line drawings on the whiteboard to show the difference between simple (one leaf) and compound (multiple leaflet) leaves. To illustrate "opposite" versus "alternate" placement of leaves along their branches, she first asks for two volunteers and lines them up facing in opposite directions. Then, to demonstrate alternating leaves, she asks my students to count off around the circle—one, two, one, two. The accompanying drawings help clarify the term *alternate*. Once the students grasp the concepts Barbara has introduced, they spend the majority of their time with her at the stream, where each group has chosen three or four trees they want to identify with Barbara's help.

In a similar fashion, over the years I have brought in experts on rocks, insects, bones, and birds (see Figure 1.3). These professionals enjoy the challenge of translating their respective disciplines into language accessible to my students and me. Fueled with the excitement of my own new understanding, I am then able to clarify, explain, or expand my students' perceptions and knowledge.

In addition to the experts, I also rely on conversations with my partner, David, a high school science teacher. Since I encourage my students to ask questions (see Chapter 2), often a question will emerge that does not warrant a whole unit of study or a special visitor. At these times I bring my students' questions to David, and we go back and forth until I understand how electricity works or why we can see the sun when gases are invisible. Then I try to take those answers back to my students.

FIGURE 1.3 - Dr. Howard Evans, a Cornell College of Veterinary Medicine professor emeritus of anatomy, shows students his collection of bird specimens, including an ostrich egg and a chicken skeleton.

If, like me, you do not easily identify yourself as a scientist or scientific thinker, I strongly recommend finding a science mentor, someone willing to be on call to guide you through confusing concepts and boost your confidence as a science teacher. If there is no obvious friend or colleague to fit the bill, call a nature center, science museum, high school or college science department, or a senior citizen center. Your questions and the ensuing conversations will usher you into the community of scientists, transform the way you experience the world, and turn science into one of your favorite subjects to teach.

TIP #7. GATHER EQUIPMENT AND TOOLS

The first time we go out to the stream we carry only our nature journals. Then with each successive visit I introduce another tool: hand lenses, collection tanks, measurement tools, field guides, and, finally, binoculars. Through the years I have used my supply budget (and applied for grant money) to purchase

FIGURE 1.4 - Each
stream study group
carries a container
of measurement and
observation tools.

more specialized equipment, but I started out with recycled plastic containers, string, meter sticks, and borrowed thermometers.

I purchase most of my equipment from the ETA hand2mind (formally ETA/Cuisenaire) science catalog. Over time their products have proved to be durable and of consistent quality. I have had the opportunity to try different models as well because, after passing through many seven- and eight-year-old hands, some tools do need to be replaced. I have enough hand lenses for each student to carry his or her own. The other tools are shared within each group.

Plastic Hand Lens Magnifiers—I drill a small hole in the plastic handle of each lens and run a piece of string through the hole to make lens "necklaces" that are not so easily lost or left behind.

Collection Tanks—I use half-gallon and gallon flex-tank aquariums with covers. They stack for efficient storage and double as terrariums. My very first collection tanks were the flat, white plastic, rectangular containers used to ship fish. Since they cannot be reused commercially, go to a local fish restaurant or supermarket and find out what time of day these containers will be thrown out.

Bug Box Magnifiers—Small plastic containers with magnifier covers are great for bringing dead insects, shells, cones, etc., into the classroom for further observation and drawing.

Tape Measures—I switched from retractable three-meter/ten-foot metal tape measures that bent and rusted to more expensive ten-meter/thirty-foot wind-up plastic tape measures. For a cheaper alternative, use string or yarn to measure long distances and then measure the string stretched across meter sticks.

Meter Sticks and Rulers—I use standard wooden meter sticks and rulers that have centimeters marked on one side and inches marked on the other.

Thermometers—I have tried metal-backed and plastic-backed student thermometers. Most are inconsistent in their temperature readings. I prefer the ones with larger numbers and scale lines.

Timers—These seem to have the shortest shelf life. I currently use the student "VersaTimers," but every once in a while I have had to send one back.

I gather together all the small tools in a basket or plastic container for each stream group to carry with them. Also included are a Ping-Pong ball or cork for measuring speed, a latex glove and plastic bag for picking up trash, a laminated sheet with drawings of aquatic invertebrates, and extra pencils (see Figure 1.4). The meter sticks and collection tanks are carried separately. At the end of each stream study I make sure that the kits are complete so that they are ready for our next visit. Everything is stored together in the closet with the outgrown rubber boots and rain ponchos donated over time.

It doesn't take long for the school community to hear about the nature study happening in your classroom, and you may be gifted with offers of tools and equipment to get you started.

TIP #8. FIND CHILDREN'S LITERATURE ABOUT THE NATURAL WORLD

One of my favorite planning tasks is choosing the books I will read to my students each week. I try to read aloud twice a day. The first book is usually a picture book—fiction, nonfiction, folktale, or poetry—completed in one to three days, depending on its complexity. The second is a longer novel that I read over a couple of months. If one day I am able to get to a third book, I always proclaim our good fortune aloud before reading. Our school year is one hundred eighty days long, so at a maximum I may get to read about two hundred fifty picture books. That is a drop in the bucket of excellent children's literature.

I have two criteria for choosing. First, I need to love the book: writing that sounds good to my ear and moves my heart for fiction and poetry; writing that is clear and concise for nonfiction; illustrations or photographs that are pleasing to the eye and enhance the text. Second, the book needs to fit in with our studies and interests. Many of my selections will inform and enrich our nature study throughout the year.

The librarian at our school has been my most valuable support system in not only finding the books I need (often requesting titles through our interlibrary loan system) but also adding to our school collection as new books are published. She helps me locate read-alouds as well as books suitable for my students to read independently. Since it is impossible for me to read them all, she often holds back a few titles that she reads to my class during our library time.

My nature read-aloud repertoire includes but is not limited to books about observation and drawing, streams, rivers, salamanders, crayfish, trout, trees, animal tracks, weather, seasonal changes, and birds. Often I search for titles that respond to my students' interests and questions or to an observation we have experienced together. Some of my favorite authors are Jim Arnosky, Byrd Baylor, Lynne Cherry, Lindsay Barrett George, Thomas Locker, Scott Russell Sanders, and Millicent E. Selsam. Many titles included in the references section are suited to nature study in any natural setting, but when a title is specific to a woodland habitat, you will often find that the same author has written books about other environments. *Around the Pond: Who's Been Here* by Lindsay Barrett George, *Crinkleroot's Guide to Knowing Animal Habitats* by Jim Arnosky, and *Mountain Dance* by Thomas Locker are just a few examples.

I also look for poems and songs that relate to our study of the natural world. Each morning we sing a song and recite a poem together. When we have mastered a song, accompanied by me on guitar, we record it on a digital recorder and move on to the next one. (At the end of the year each student receives a CD of all the songs we have learned.) In the fall, standards are "Walk Outside" by Raffi and "Ain't No Bugs on Me," a traditional folk song. In the spring we sing "Sakura," a Japanese folk song about cherry blossoms; "Habitat" by Tom Knight; and the "Leaf Cutter Ants' Parade," sung to the tune of "When Johnny Comes Marching Home."

The poems of Kristine O'Connell George and Anna Grossnickle Hines are at the top of my list. They are short enough to memorize but also rich in poetic imagery. Later in the year I will use their poems as models for my second graders when they begin to write poems of their own. It is thrilling when my students make connections between the poems we memorize together and the natural world we explore. "Look! The leaves are dancing," they shout after we have memorized "Rock and Roll" by Grossnickle Hines (2008). When we go out to the stream, they spontaneously start reciting, "That tree across the stream is a trickier bridge than it might seem" by O'Connell George (1998, 14).

Last but not least, every year I order more field guides, six copies of one title, for my classroom library. The field guides cover whatever we might find at the stream or whatever my students might discover at home—caterpillars, moths and butterflies, insects, reptiles and amphibians, clouds, trees, wildflowers, mammals, and birds. I started with a beginner series—Peterson's First Guides or Stokes Beginner's Guides—but I am slowly adding adult guides as well (see Chapter 6).

TIP #9. TEACH YOUR STUDENTS HOW TO USE NATURE JOURNALS

I usually share pages from some of my own nature journals within the first week of the new school year. The pages I choose illustrate the variety of possible entries. I show two entries from a hike around Mount Rainier—a drawing of a magenta paintbrush flower (see Figure 1.5), an animal footprint with recorded

FIGURE 1.5 - I try out whatever I ask my students to do, in this case a drawing of a magenta paintbrush flower from a hike around Mount Rainier.

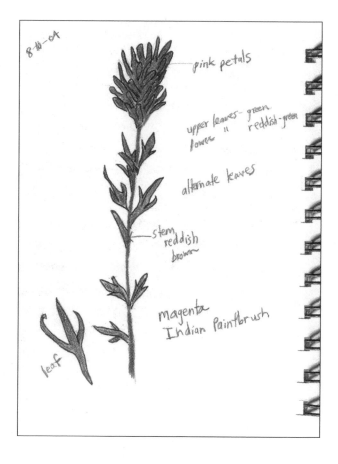

measurements—and then a list of questions I had one day about squirrel nests. I reveal that they will soon be getting their own nature journals too.

"Why do you like nature so much?" asks Shannon.

"What a great question, Shannon," I respond as I scroll through all the possible answers I could give. I realize that no one has ever asked me this question before.

"I guess what I love most is that when I observe the natural world carefully, I see and hear things I never used to notice before—the birds singing or the smallest insects crawling on the ground. And when I notice, I feel like I'm surrounded by friends and that makes me happy."

I look straight at Shannon, who smiles back at me with a slight nod of her head. It is at this moment that I gently release my connection to last year's students and embrace the group sitting in front of me. I am ready to follow these children down a new path of learning and discovery in the natural world.

A week later I introduce their special nature journals. I explored many possibilities and decided that blank pages were a priority since I want to encourage drawing as much as writing. Every year I splurge and use most of my supply budget to buy real artist sketchbooks (Strathmore spiral-bound drawing pads, 6 by 8 inches, twenty-four pages) that have a stiff cardboard backing to lean on in the field. That said, I want to be clear that this option is not critical. Composition notebooks, stenographer's pads, or journals made with shirt-cardboard covers, typing-paper pages, and bound with paper fasteners are practical, economical, and effective.

FIGURE 1.6 - Students choose magazine photos to decorate their nature journal covers.

FIGURE 1.7 - A sampling of completed nature journals covered with clear contact paper.

I show the cover of my school nature journal, identical to theirs, and then pass out brand-new journals to my students with great fanfare. We spend an hour decorating our covers. Each table is covered with newspaper and supplied with scissors, glue sticks, old magazines (*Ranger Rick, World, Living Bird, Bird and Blooms*) and garden catalogs. Their job is to make a collage of pictures on the cover of their journals. Every single student is engaged (see Figure 1.6). Although one student cuts out Sponge Bob and another cuts out pictures of race cars, most stick to animals and plants, looking for their favorites—koala bears, cats, dogs, or killer whales. The finishing touch is a white label on which they write their names. I have already arranged for parent volunteers to cover these colorful masterpieces with clear contact paper to protect them from a light rain (see Figure 1.7).

Parent volunteers will also complete a journal page for each stream visit, modeling aloud for the students in their groups as they write and draw their entries. I use whatever is on hand for the parent journals, such as composition notebooks, and these journals last several years.

On the day of our first stream study, parents show up early, before the students return from recess. Their faces look eager, just like their children's. Bella helps me put colored dots on their nature journals so that they can be easily sorted into the three stream groups—Red, Blue and Green.

As soon as my students are gathered on the rug, I start speaking in a quiet voice filled with a sense of wonder.

"When you draw or write in a nature journal, you will start to look at the world with new eyes. A nature journal will help you make friends with the plants and animals at your secret sit spot. As you start to explore, you can record what you see, smell, hear, feel, and think in words or pictures. You can add labels and color your pictures. You can write poems or make up stories about your new friends. You will always remember what you write and draw about."

Then I turn to more practical considerations.

"Thumbs up if you have a special way to draw flowers. Thumbs up if you have a special way that you always draw trees. In your nature journals you will do a very special kind of drawing. You will try to draw exactly what you see."

I demonstrate how I draw a stereotypical flower or tree and then how I might draw flowers and trees that I am observing closely. Our art teacher, upon my request, has already introduced the difference between observational drawing and drawing from your imagination.

"Today I want you to choose something at the stream to look at very closely and make a drawing in your journal. I also want you to think of a question you have about what you see."

I establish our first journaling routine and model how to enter the date and weather on the top of their journal pages. Then, journals and pencils in hand, we line up at the door, eager to write and draw about our new friends in the natural world.

Peter draws a fungus and roots and writes, "Why is it black? What kind of plant was it?" (see Figure 1.8). Julius draws a salamander and a cocoon and writes, "I found this salamander in the stream under a rock. I wonder what this cocoon is" (see Figure 1.9). Shannon draws a spider and writes, "Question:

FIGURE 1.8 - Peter takes the time to draw what he sees before he records his questions.

What kind of spider is it? Where: under a rock. How big: inch to inch and a half. How it moves: feels with front legs and moves with all eight."

TIP #10. PRIME YOUR STUDENTS FOR A YEAR OF NATURE STUDY

I want my students to start noticing the world around them with new eyes. From the first day of school I am on the lookout for wildlife outside our classroom window. We look out on a small wood with mown lawn in the foreground where I can count on a variety of creatures to show up throughout the year. I depend on the gray squirrels, chipmunks, deer, cottontail rabbits, turkeys, songbirds, and the occasional hawk or woodchuck to guide my students toward careful observation and thoughtful questioning.

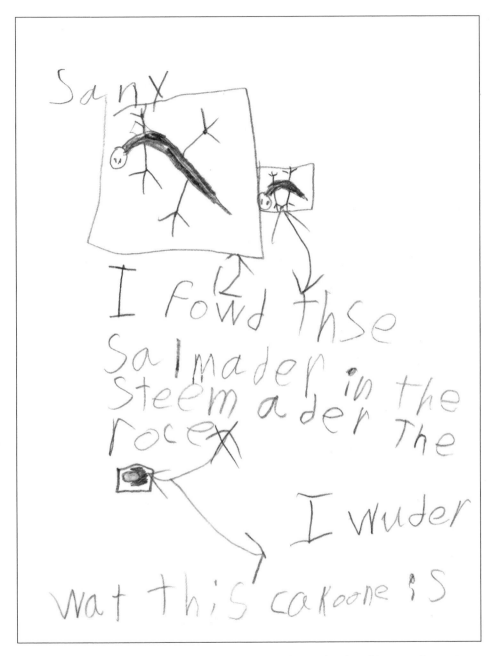

FIGURE 1.9 - Julius draws a stick figure salamander and writes his question using invented spelling.

Observation

You can reach the same goal by bringing something into the classroom to observe—a caterpillar, a spider, a piece of bark, a shell collection, some well-rotted compost, or a houseplant. You can invite your students to bring in their own finds in the natural world or small pets to share and observe—turtles, hamsters, fish (see Figure 1.10). After we study an animal together for the first time, I introduce the terms *features* and *behaviors,* and we chart our observations under those rubrics (see Chapter 7).

At first it is important to value all observations. Later you can begin to help your students differentiate between objective observations (he's curling into a ball) and subjective opinions (he's cute).

Thursday, September 4, second day of school

I am in the middle of explaining our first handwriting practice when I notice two fawns at the edge of the woods outside our classroom window. I can feel a gentle rush of excitement glide through me. Our year of nature study is off and running. I finish my presentation on capital letters and without skipping a beat I announce softly, "Please stand up and walk very quietly and slowly to the windows. What do you see?" I continue to whisper, "very slowly," and everyone complies.

Within a few seconds, everyone spots the deer, young ones but already four feet high. "Observe very carefully, raise your hand, and tell me what you notice." The first response is obvious.

"They have spots," declares Rachel.

"Great start," I reply. "Now keep noticing. What are they doing?"

"They're eating." offers Jose.

"Good. What are they eating?"

"Grass."

"What else?"

"Leaves."

Soon the responses become more detailed, and I try to comment on each one.

"They don't have spots along their spines," Ivan points out.

"I didn't notice that, Ivan. I'm going to try to look for that from now on. Thank you for observing so closely."

"They have big ears," suggests Stella.

"Their ears can move forward, backward, and sideways," adds Julius.

Realizing that only those nearby can hear Julius, I get everyone's attention and ask him to repeat what he noticed about the ears. This is the kind of observation I want my students to make, and I want to be sure everyone hears it.

"Let's watch and see what that looks like. When you look very carefully, this is the kind of observation you can make. How do the big ears help the deer?"

After a brief discussion about listening and predators, Margot points out, "Their legs go backward." We all take in how their "knees" bend in the opposite direction of ours.

"I'm noticing that the deer stay mostly at the edge of the woods. Why do you think they do that?" I ask. Shannon raises her hand immediately. "If something is after them, they can run into the woods and hide."

In ten minutes my students receive their first lesson in making friends in the natural world, and we return to our handwriting practice.

FIGURE 1.10 - Early in September a student shares a woolly bear caterpillar, the larval stage of the Isabella tiger moth.

Asking Questions
Monday morning, September 15

We are in the middle of writing workshop when Luke notices the birds. Oh dear, I'm thinking. We're not going to start an in-depth bird study until November. But when I go over to look, I know I cannot let this one go. There must be one hundred blackbirds on the grass.

Without my binoculars I am not sure if they are starlings or grackles. They look more like starlings (some are browner or more speckled than others), but the tails look too long. Once again I am humbled at how often I need to refresh my own knowledge.

I invite the rest of the class to come slowly to the window and take a look. Since we are not into bird identification yet, I start in on what I hope will be the focus for the year. "What questions are popping up in your mind? What are you wondering about them?" I ask.

"What are they?" Davey asks.

"Why are they here?" wonders Peter.

A few other students repeat, "What are they?" in different words, and I end with, "Why are there so many altogether?" I am already thinking ahead to when we will be talking about migration, and I can refer to this time of the birds flocking in the fall.

At some point, someone asks me about stream study. I tell the class that we will go out this week, on Wednesday. Peter, whose brother Charlie I taught four years earlier, puts up both thumbs as he pulls back his elbows.

"Yesss!" he exclaims.

It is *that* cool to have stream study. We are on our way!

MAKE NATURE STUDY YOUR OWN

There you have it—ten tips for getting started with nature study.

There are *logistics* to work through (Tips #2–4):

- **Fitting nature study into your weekly schedule**
- **Choosing a "secret" sit spot**
- **Safety considerations**

Materials to gather and *resources* to identify (Tips #5–8):

- **Volunteers to recruit**
- **Community experts to engage**
- **Tools and equipment to acquire**
- **Children's literature to collect**

Discussions and *activities* to engage your students (Tips #9–10):

- **Nature journals**
- **Getting your students ready**

Most important, be sure to take your time with the first tip and *become a naturalist yourself*. Start with what *you* love about the natural world—the smell of lilacs in the spring, picnicking in a local park, waking up on a glorious sunny morning, an annual pilgrimage to your favorite beach, the delightful surprise of a rainbow, walking your dog in the woods, a full moon, working in your garden, or gazing at the sunset from your front porch. It is not necessary to become a full-fledged naturalist. Your specific knowledge about invertebrates, rock formations, or invasive species is not as important as your comfort level out of doors and your delight in a particular corner of your world. Remind yourself of what you love about nature and use that passion to engage your students.

It is also not necessary to start with a yearlong, fully integrated nature study. You can begin at any time of the year and also get your feet wet (literally or not!) with a single trip to a local park or nature center. Try connecting to another teacher to brainstorm ideas or become nature study buddies. A fifth-grade class exploring the natural world with a class of kindergartners just might provide the right number of extra hands.

In the meantime, take a summer or take a year until you start to experience your world with all of your senses. Before nature study, I barely noticed the robins on my front lawn. Now I listen for their birdsong in my first waking moments. I can identify male and female robins by the subtle difference in their colors. I look forward to the fledging of the juvenile birds and their teenage behavior so unlike their parents.

When the smallest flicker of movement in your peripheral vision catches your attention or you find yourself pulling the car over to the side of the road to crane your neck at some bird on the telephone wire, you will probably be ready to introduce your students to the natural world. Then you will sashay through the remaining nine tips, and you too will be on your way!

CHAPTER 2

Moments of Science

I first heard about "moments of science" when my partner, David, and I were sharing our daily teaching stories in early September. I would often rely on his knowledge as a high school science teacher (and former biotechnology laboratory researcher) when I was trying to distill the most important teaching points in a science lesson. While I knew that science was compelling for my seven- and eight-year-old second graders, I was still trying to figure out how to make *teaching* science compelling for me. On that notable day in September, David was telling me about a student in his class who had earned a "moment of science" for discovering a mistake in the physics textbook.

David developed this practice of honoring moments of science over time. It started one day when he did not immediately know the answer to a student's question in class and found that when he returned with the answer a few days later, his student had already forgotten the question. David realized that, as a teacher, finding the answer was not as important as his student's asking the question. He was trying to teach his students to think like scientists and asking the question is exactly what science is all about. The next time a question emerged, he wanted to call attention to it; he wanted his students to pay attention to this kind of thinking when it happened to them. It turned out that David's students, motivated by his high regard for their innovative ideas and questions, considered it an honor to "make the board," the auxiliary chalkboard where he would jot down the names, dates, and a few words to identify their brainstorms. His students were always on the lookout for someone who deserved a "moment." I was eager to try out this practice with mine.

The day I started celebrating moments of science was the day I started to get excited about *teaching* science. I finally understood, from the inside out, what it meant to have an inquiry-based science curriculum. I continued to teach the required curriculum but within that framework, my students were free to generate their own questions, and together we could wander off the beaten path to research, experiment, hypothesize, and think as a community of scientists.

By the mid-nineties, "inquiry-based" curriculum had become the touted best practice for teaching science in my school district. Soon science kits complete with all necessary materials appeared outside our doors, and we were told to create inquiry-based lessons. We attended special training sessions to learn how to use the kits and present their prepackaged inquiry questions to our students. We learned how to use the kits but not how to feel comfortable teaching science, and our students did not develop inquiring minds.

I firmly believe that programs and kits do not teach students. Teachers teach students. If we do not understand the scientific principles behind a lesson, if we do not deepen our own scientific understanding, then we are reduced to reading a script that will not engage our students in meaningful inquiry. The kits' manuals cannot trigger their innate curiosity or spark their sense of wonder about the world.

I found my comfort zone using moments of science. This teaching practice released me from needing an immediate answer to any question. It relaxed my fears and, even more important, wiped out my reluctance to teach unfamiliar material. Instead, my own "inner scientist" began to come alive. I began to look forward to my students' questions as an opportunity to expand my own scientific thinking and understanding.

Over time, the pulse of my classroom changed. One splendid day I realized that my students and I were living and breathing that once-elusive concept called *inquiry*. We were working our way through the principles of the scientific method—meandering back and forth between observation, asking questions, making hypotheses, looking for evidence, and drawing conclusions. Whether I

FIGURE 2.1 - Sophie draws the tree that inspires her revelation: "trees are not really brown, they are gray."

was teaching the required scientific curriculum in the classroom or taking my students outside to explore the natural world, moments of science provided a framework to encourage my students as well as their teacher to think like scientists.

EARNING MOMENTS OF SCIENCE

Sophie is drawing in her journal on our first stream visit of the year. "Laurie," she pauses to make sure she has my attention, "most people make trees brown but they're not" (see Figure 2.1).

"What color are they?" I ask.

"Kind of grayish," she responds. I get goose bumps because it has been eight years since I had the same revelation when I was sitting in a local state park attempting to draw a tree. It was the first time I had looked at something for a whole hour trying to record every detail. After getting the outline of the tree down, I took out my colored pencils. At that moment, as I tried to find the right color for the bark, I realized, like Sophie, that some tree trunks are gray. Now, sitting next to Sophie, I marvel at the magic of sustained observation that can change the world for someone at any age, seven or forty-seven.

Sophie earns a moment of science for her epiphany. Moments of science in my classroom celebrate critical thinking skills—a thoughtful question, observation, hypothesis, or conclusion. Early in the year, I always explain to my young students that scientists move around their world in a very special way—they look very carefully, they are always asking questions, and they try to figure out how things work. Then I try to give my students many opportunities to observe and question *their* worlds. (See Chapter 1, Tip #10.)

Each year I wait eagerly for the first moment of science to reveal itself. Three years ago it was Sophie's tree. Another year it happens when Austin brings a snakeskin to share with the class. When he opens his shoebox, Téo shouts out, "That's not a snake skin."

We let Austin finish his share, and I suggest that we can all take a closer look at the skin on our way to gym.

An hour later, the children line up, and I take the shoebox from Austin. As soon as I open it, I realize Téo is correct—this is a flattened-out snake, not a snakeskin.

"You know, Austin, I think Téo might be right," I say calmly. "Usually when snakes shed their skin, it's clear or transparent and it looks kind of white. This looks like a snake that was stepped on or run over by a bicycle."

"My mother said it was a snakeskin," Austin responds with a son's unshakable faith in his mother's knowledge.

Hmmm. As I ponder how to answer delicately, I notice a tiny piece of skin on the edge of the snake. When I point it out, Austin doesn't skip a beat.

"Maybe the snake started to shed its skin and *then* it got run over."

Right there, lined up to go to gym, I honor Austin's moment of science.

"Molting certainly slows an animal down so maybe the snake didn't have time to slither away. What good thinking, Austin."

This year it happens when I read *Crinkleroot's Guide to Knowing the Trees* by Jim Arnosky, a self-taught writer, artist, and naturalist. Arnosky explains that when a tree falls down, an open space is created where sunlight can pour down and new saplings can grow. I read on about animals like grouse and wild turkey that like to eat in the warm sun, yet stay close to the woods in case they need cover.

Julius raises his hand. I read one more page before calling on him.

"That answers our question about the turkeys," he announces.

It takes me a few seconds to realize what he is talking about. Last week a flock of turkeys appeared on the grass behind the school—not right in front of our window but close enough to observe for a while. We did the usual—shared our observations and asked questions. One of the questions was, "Why are the turkeys here?" meaning on the grass. Now Julius has made a connection between our question and the information in Arnosky's book.

"Remember the turkeys on the grass last week?" I ask. "Julius just realized that *our* turkeys must have been enjoying the warm sunshine but staying close to the woods in case of danger. Julius, you just made a great connection *and* you earned yourself a moment of science.

"A moment of science in our class celebrates thinking questions and hypotheses," I explain upon awarding the first moment of the year. "That means your ideas about the world and your observations. A moment of science celebrates wondering about how things work. Julius had a moment of science for our *class*. He noticed that our *turkey* question was answered in this book about *trees*. What a surprise!

"You can also have your own moments of science at home and record them in your nature journal. Then you will remember your second-grade questions, ideas, and discoveries for the rest of your lives."

I read the last few pages of the book, take out a 6-by-18-inch strip of yellow construction paper, and write the heading, "Moments of Science." Underneath I write, "October 8—Julius finds the answer to our turkey question." Throughout the school year, I will continue to record our moments of science. They will stay on the board next to the calendar until June, when I type them up and post them for posterity, to inspire my future students, and me.

In fact, when I first mention moments of science, Laura points to the wall where all the moments of science from previous years are typed and posted. I walk over to what I call the Moments of Science Hall of Fame and read aloud a few moments earned by older siblings. In February 2006, Rosie's sister Annie asked, "How do birds know where to migrate?" In April 2007, Aurora's brother

Edward thought that, "When carnivores eat herbivores, they are getting the nutrients in plants." My students listen intently, perhaps wondering if some day their names will be up there too (see Figure 2.2).

OBSERVING AND ASKING QUESTIONS

This year we are participating in a national program called Trout in the Classroom (TIC). This program seemed like a perfect addition to our stream study since our little stream (and dry streambed!) would never support fish.

On October 14, TIC coordinator Bill Foster and Trout Unlimited member Chris Stull come after school to set up the trout tank. The next day, as my students arrive one by one, they join the crowd in front of the tank. They cannot resist running their fingers through the condensed water on the glass and are

FIGURE 2.2 - The Moments of Science Hall of Fame list is posted in the classroom.

surprised to find out that the water inside the tank is cold. I explain that we are creating a habitat for wild trout that live in cold streams and rivers.

Two days later, before leaving school for the day, I raise the chiller setting from 55°F to 70°F. We will save energy until the trout eggs are delivered at the end of October.

The next morning, Margot is the first to notice that, "the fog is gone." The water condensation on the outside of the fish tank has vanished. I ask why and Aurora answers, "It dried up from the heat." Julius starts in on a complicated explanation about evaporation and settles for, "It happens with a glass of water."

I start madly searching through the pile of weather books I collected in preparation for a new FOSS Air and Weather science kit I will be implementing for the first time. I want to take advantage of this magical moment, but I know I am not well versed in the physical sciences. I find *Where Do Puddles Go?*—a Rookie Read-About Science Book—which has a simple explanation of the water cycle. When the whole class arrives, I read about water vapor and how it condenses when the air gets cooler. We pause to remember the condensed water on the fish tank when the water was set at 55°F. When the 70°F air in the room hit the fish tank at 55°F, the water vapor condensed on the cooler glass. When I raised the water temperature to match room temperature, the "heat," as Aurora suggested, turned the condensed droplets of water back into invisible water vapor.

This firsthand experience with water condensation and evaporation would never have happened without my students' developing observation skills and natural curiosity. In the hectic pace of a second-grade classroom, I am certain that I would never have noticed the disappearance of the "fog." And now, each time I sit down behind the steering wheel of my car and turn on the windshield wipers to clear away the condensation, I remember the fog on the trout tank and understand the water cycle "from the inside out."

Then, on October 30, we eagerly receive one hundred brown trout eggs and watch them hatch into alevins. Alevins have yolk sacs that provide all the nourishment needed for the first few weeks of the fish's life. When the egg sacs are used up, the alevins turn into fingerlings or fry (juvenile trout), and we begin weekly feedings of meal in addition to monitoring tank water quality. Seated in front of the fifty-gallon trout tank, we have many opportunities to practice our observation and questioning skills as we watch the fry grow (see Figure 2.3).

FIGURE 2.3 - The trout tank provides opportunities for observation and critical thinking.

❖   ❖   ❖

Two weeks later, I read to my class from the Air and Weather manual, "Air is a form of matter. There are three kinds of matter: solids, liquids, and gases. Air is an invisible mixture of gases." We are just clearing up the difference between *invisible* and *indivisible*, one of the many mystery words in the Pledge of Allegiance I have recently explained, when Julius raises his hand.

"Laurie, is electricity a gas?"

"I don't know, Julius. I'll have to talk to a scientist, and I guess you just earned yourself another moment of science."

"But he already got one," Jasmine points out.

I too am conflicted about giving him another one so soon (only two moments have been awarded so far this year and Julius earned the first one) and, although stumping the teacher (which he has!) is not a prerequisite for earning a "moment," this way of wondering about the world is exactly what I want to value in my classroom.

"I know, Jasmine, but I just can't ignore this good thinking."

All of a sudden six hands are in the air.

Hannah is trying to say something about how solids are different from each other. After a few exchanges back and forth, I uncover the idea she is pondering: some solids such as paper can bend and some such as wood cannot bend. She earns a moment of science.

It is all flying so fast and furiously, I cannot remember every nuance but somehow we are talking about space and the sun and the big bang and then someone wants to know if there is air in outer space. I erroneously answer, "Yes, but there is no oxygen."

"If the sun is a gas and gases are invisible, why can we see the sun?" Rosie wants to know (see Figure 2.4).

Bingo—another moment of science and more research for me because, again, I do not know how to answer. (Although I do not always bring answers back to my students, in this case my own curiosity is aroused.) More hands go up. I have already bequeathed three moments of science in less than ten minutes, and there are clearly more critical thinkers out there waiting their turns. But it is time to go to gym. I promise to listen to one more on the way.

Shannon asks, "If birds are solid, why can they fly?" Finally I know the answer, but I hold it back.

"We will find out when we study birds, Shannon, but you can go home and do some research on your own if you want to find out now." I will give Shannon a moment of science as well (see Chapter 8).

As I walk back to my classroom, I am totally energized by a discussion that flew from three kinds of matter to electricity, properties of solids, outer space, the sun, and birds. The critical thinking skills we have practiced through nature study are transforming the required science curriculum. I am eager to talk to David tonight and get answers to all these questions. As it turns out, the answers are complex and not so easy for me to wrap my brain around. It takes a few different conversations before I feel confident enough to report back to

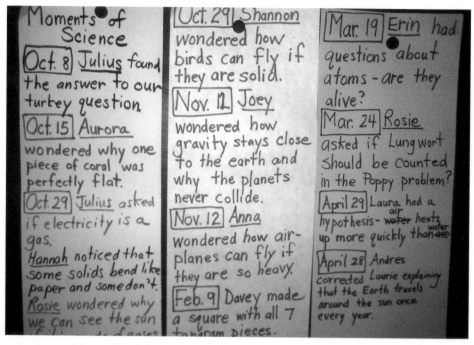

FIGURE 2.4 - Moments of Science are recorded and displayed at the front of the classroom as they occur.

my students. I also make sure to confess that I was wrong about outer space having any air.

Once again my students challenge me to stretch my scientific understanding and to walk around my world with new awareness. I realize that a vibrant community of scientists is starting to form in our second-grade classroom. The climate of inquiry created together is invigorating. Using moments of science, we are ready to continue our investigation of the scientific process.

MAKING HYPOTHESES

I don't always recognize moments of science when they first occur. Once you start thinking this way, it becomes easier to spot them, but it is always fine to revisit them after the fact. In Sophie's case, it actually took me a week to realize she belonged on the board!

I also try to be conscious of "copycat" moments. The first year I introduced moments of science, it was one afternoon after recess when Lucas brought in a maple leaf with an extremely long stem. It was quite impressive, measuring twenty-nine centimeters long. He earned a moment of science for his excellent observation skills. The next day ten students brought in long-stemmed leaves from the playground. I examined each leaf carefully and celebrated each student's increasing awareness of the natural world, but they did not qualify for moments of science.

I also have to be prepared for these moments to arise at inconvenient times. One brisk September day, in the middle of a discussion about how to turn weather data into a graph, Abigail raises her hand.

"Every time I look out the window, I see a squirrel in the exact same place," she declares with an audible "hmmm" in her voice.

Instead of reprimanding her for being off topic, I go with it.

"What a great observation, Abigail. Why do you think that squirrel is always in the same spot?" (I decide it is time to add the concept of hypothesis to our naturalist tool belts.) "What is your hypothesis?"

It takes measurable wait time but finally she answers, cautiously.

"Maybe its home is nearby?"

Many more hands shoot up with possibilities:

"Maybe it's the home of a squirrel friend?"

"Maybe squirrels are burying acorns there?"

"Maybe squirrels are digging them up?"

"Maybe acorns are falling from a tree in exactly that spot?"

Abigail earns a moment, and I take the opportunity to reinforce the idea that when scientists notice something, they always ask, "What is going on here?" and they try to make a guess or hypothesis. In less than five minutes we are back into graphing.

Exactly two months later, as we are cleaning up the classroom at the end of the day, Emily comes up to me and says, "I think Abigail was right about the squirrel. I saw a squirrel go into that hole."

Emily earns a moment of science too, but why don't I consider this one another copycat moment? It was only after talking it through with David that I could affirm my gut feeling that Emily's observation—the squirrel down the hole—was, in fact, unique. Emily's hypothesis connects to the one Abigail made two months earlier. Emily is not only adding evidence for Abigail's hypothesis (the hole is close to where Abigail saw the squirrel) but also observing that same spot over time, in a sense replicating Abigail's observation. Emily earns a moment of science because she is participating in a simple, oral form of scientific peer review, whereby scientists evaluate and confirm the published research of a colleague by trying to replicate the results.

In February, Bill Foster returns with *Daphnia magnus,* a species of freshwater zooplankton that provides a food source in natural systems for many juvenile fish. We will find out whether *our* trout recognize these nearly microscopic animals as a natural food source. It turns into an ideal moment to work on making hypotheses.

We break up into our stream groups and Bill removes several trout for each group to observe in small containers. First, my group makes these observations:

Features—red gills, black parr marks, clear fins, seven fins plus tail

Behaviors—gills flapping open, mouth moving

Next, Bill introduces zooplankton into each container. We watch for three minutes, recording how many zooplankton are consumed every ten seconds. It turns out that most of the trout eat nothing. By now, thinking about "why" is a habit and, with no prompting, my students offer their hypotheses.

Joey: The trout aren't used to their habitat.

Anna: The trout are concentrating on trying to get out of the habitat.

Hannah: The people are distracting the trout. They are more interested in us than in the zooplankton.

Ariella: They are lonely.

Bill thinks that the bigger trout (he tried introducing zooplankton at other schools when the trout were smaller) are more skittish, more aware of danger, and do not adapt to the new environment.

At the end of the school day, I have time to reflect on our zooplankton experience. My students were able to use their observation skills in a new way, record data for authentic purposes, hypothesize instinctively, and learn that experiments do not always work. What could have been a failed activity turns into an opportunity for my students to practice their critical thinking skills and learn even more about the scientific process.

LOOKING FOR EVIDENCE

In early March, we begin to have a new flurry of shares from the natural world. Spring is in the air, and my students are spending more time outdoors again. Laura brings in a stick she found with her sister. The bark is off and very small holes are visible in a regular pattern along the stick. There are also markings on the stick that look like somebody drew some lines. When Laura asks for comments and questions, Rachel suggests that a woodpecker made the holes. Joey says insects made the holes, and Peter thinks maybe all sticks look like that under the bark.

I ask whether anyone has evidence or proof to support his or her hypothesis. Rachel says she has seen woodpeckers pecking on branches like that. Julius tells us that the lines look just like the ones he saw at the nature center on some trees, and the naturalist said that insects make those lines. Although I go on to value all the hypotheses, I conclude that Julius's experience was convincing evidence—that a naturalist is an expert whom we can trust.

A week later Margot brings in a skull. Most of the students who ask questions want to know what kind of skull it is. A bird?

"No," Margot answers. "I don't see a beak."

I get up, stand next to Margot, and turn over the skull so that we can see a row of teeth. I turn to the class and ask which animal could *not* have a skull like this. I explain that often scientists first try to eliminate what is *not* possible.

A chipmunk is the first reply so I reiterate that scientists would first try to eliminate what it cannot be. "Which animals do *not* have teeth?" I ask.

"It couldn't be a bird."

"It couldn't be a snake." Joey, our resident snake expert, takes a look and confirms that the teeth are not sharp enough to be a snake's.

Now Margot says it might be a squirrel skull because there is a squirrel at her house that is always bothering them with loud noises. She saw it go under the porch and that's where she found the skull.

We affirm that the place you find something gives you important information.

Luke thinks it might be a cat skull because he sees cats going under porches. Andres also thinks it is a squirrel skull because it looks like the ones he has from the nature center. They were giving away skulls and there was a sign above them that said "squirrel."

I turn to the class and say, "thumbs up if you would trust the nature center staff to know what a squirrel skull looks like." Most thumbs go up. I ask Margot if she can leave her skull in school until Andres can bring in one of his skulls next week. They both agree, and we make a plan to revisit the skull question.

It seems that the more I value the various rocks and sticks and feathers that appear each week, the more other students join in the conversation and bring in shares of their own.

❋ ❋ ❋

It is mid-March and we are a month into writing poetry. We decide to write a class poem about the trout fingerlings. When I take off the foam cover in front of the tank, we find all the trout on the bottom of the tank. Someone asks if it is good or bad that they are all on the bottom, and then we make our hypotheses. This time we try to give evidence to prove our ideas.

Ariella: It's good because the water is colder down there; it might be warmer on the top because of the warmth in the room.

Joey: It's good because when we release them in the wild, they're gonna stay on the bottom and it's gonna be harder for birds or other predators that attack from above to get them.

Hannah: I thought that when Bill and Chris [from Trout Unlimited] came, they said that when they're on the bottom, that they're unhappy or something, or is it the opposite?

Rachel: Maybe they're just scared since Bill took away some of the fish [to give to another school who lost so many], they might be scared we're gonna take them away.

Margot: It's bad for them because once you said if they're on the bottom, it means the water is a tiny bit too base. [Margot is thinking about the ammonia level.]

Aurora: Since the water is a little warmer than usual, down deep it's colder.

Julius: I think because at the bottom, there's rocks, they can camouflage in, and sometimes there's little "rests" of food that come down, and then they can eat.

At this point in the school year, our discussions are efficient. Seven- and eight-year-olds listen to each other respectfully and try to add new information to our developing understanding of the world. More students are joining in our discussions and more students are learning to back up their ideas with evidence. Our community of scientists continues to grow.

DRAWING CONCLUSIONS AS A COMMUNITY OF SCIENTISTS

"There's a new bird," Margot cries as we return to our classroom from the gym. We all rush to the windows and Ben asks if he can use his binoculars (see Figure 2.5). Sure enough, there are seven finches on the feeder. Rachel is the first to respond to my question, What do you notice?

"They're kind of brownish."

FIGURE 2.5 - Students regularly observe birds at our classroom feeder.

Julius notices that they sit right on the feeder while they are eating and the seed shells are coming out of their beaks. We take some time to see for ourselves. Julius insists they are goldfinches, but I am not sure. Davey is the only one who sees some yellow. My first thought was *house finches*. I happen to turn around, see the time, and we rush off to lunch. House finch, goldfinch, and female red-winged blackbird are our best guesses.

Five days later we have a snow day and I am at home taking the laundry out of the dryer. As I open the dryer door, movement outside catches my eye and I see the backyard is full of birds. It is 3:00 p.m., and I am never usually home at this time. I quickly count eight juncos, the most I have ever seen in my yard. There are also four finches on the thistle feeder; the exact birds we have been seeing at school.

I think back to our sightings. Every time Julius shouts out, "goldfinches," I resist and insist that we report on features and behaviors instead. The truth is I am confused. I do not remember female goldfinches having streaked breasts during winter. But then only weeks ago I realized that the males do not have black caps in winter. I grab my binoculars and, for the first time, I can see what Davey saw with his naked eye, the telltale yellow right below the finch's wing. Three streaked females and one very obvious male goldfinch. So Julius is right after all?

A week later, during recess, I log on to the All About Birds website managed by the Cornell Lab of Ornithology. There are no streaks on any goldfinch breast, summer or winter! I look through all our field guides again and settle on the pine siskin as the most likely candidate. What makes this study so gripping for me is that I continue to learn. My students can watch me learning and questioning right along with them.

After recess, I gather my students on the rug and hold up the *Stokes Beginner's Guide to Birds: Eastern Region*. Aurora has reminded me that the Stokes field guide is organized by color.

"What would you say is the main color of the new bird we have been seeing at the feeder?" I begin.

We agree to start with the brown section. One by one, we go through all thirty photographs. When there are some takers for the fox sparrow, the dissenters offer their evidence.

"The tail is too long."

"There's no black and white on the wing."

"It doesn't look right on the map," adds Anna.

Anna introduces a new kind of evidence. We take a closer look at the North American fox sparrow map. Yellow represents the summer residence, blue is winter, and green is year-round. New York State is pure white. We learn that the fox sparrow summers in Canada; it winters south of New York. It is possible that it is migrating through New York, but for now we eliminate the fox sparrow.

We reject the house finch because its beak is too round, the female red-winged blackbird because the body shape is too long and narrow, and the song sparrow because of the spot on its breast. By the time we get to the birds of prey and the waterbirds, there is a steady chorus of "nos."

When I turn the page to a bluebird, we are finished, and now I finally suggest the pine siskin, reminding everyone about Davey's seeing some yellow. We look at photos in two different field guides and read the pine siskin information: comes to feeders; often travels with goldfinches; year-round resident in New York State.

"I'm still not sure it *is* a pine siskin. I am going to ask an expert to help us. The Cornell Lab of Ornithology has an expert named Anne Hobbs, who answers questions about birds. I will send her an e-mail after school today, and we'll see what she says."

In fact, our mystery bird is indeed a pine siskin. We find out that it is an "irruptive" species—one that does not appear every year. When it does make a showing, it is often seen with goldfinches.

My students and I have come together as a community of scientists. We make observations over time. We use tools (binoculars and field guides) to make hypotheses—in this case about our mystery bird. We use evidence to eliminate possibilities and consult with an expert before drawing a conclusion. Together we share the excitement, the insights, and the give and take of a vigorous debate. Throughout this learning process, my students' contributions are equal in importance to my own.

MOMENTS OF SCIENCE AT HOME

It's the last day of school, the last half hour. The walls in my classroom are bare. Just yesterday, every chart, list, and poster generated together was spread out on the muddy brown carpet along with plastic baggies filled with pencil stubs

and broken crayons, coloring books from the U.S. Postal Service and other ac-
cumulated freebies for the "big giveaway." (The Moments of Science list is the
only one I keep.) This yearly closure ritual shows me what was important to my
students, what made an impact. Each student steps up to choose something to
take home—the 130 spelling words printed in black marker on twenty sheets
of white oak tag, the hellos and good-byes in different languages, the inven-
tory of writing craft, the strategies we brainstormed for two-digit addition
and subtraction, the cut-paper mural of the stream made in September, or
the list of birds that came to our feeder—and what they choose is significant.
No surprise that Grace and Jacob choose everything to do with birds, but who
would have guessed that Monica, a struggling math student, would go for the
addition strategies?

We have just ended our collective summer birthday party. I have asked my
students to line up so I can say good-bye to them. I know this takes a while and
I am hoping a half hour will be enough. Parents start to hover in the doorway
to say good-bye as well or to pick up their children a bit early on the last day.
I look each student in the eye and try to tell something that I know about him
or her, something I will remember. I try to be honest.

"Téo, I'm so glad you were my student this year. Your interest and excitement
about the natural world was so helpful to us. You were always looking out the
window, and although it drove me crazy sometimes, if it weren't for you, we
never would have been able to observe the pileated woodpecker so often.

"Sarah, you learned so much this year—you were already a skilled writer and
reader when you started second grade, but you tried out every new piece of
writing craft and your stories became more and more vivid. You learned how
to talk about books, and you made amazing inferences.

"Katie, you worked so hard to be a good friend this year. It wasn't easy for
you, but I noticed that you were always willing to try new strategies. You started
to have more fun on the playground."

I never know which good-bye will choke me up or which student will unexpectedly become teary-eyed. All of a sudden it is five minutes until dismissal
and I have three students to go. As I try to do them justice, I notice that Annelise has never joined the line. She is making slow circles on the floor, head
down. I try to catch her eye, but she never looks in my direction. By now the
bell has rung, and I need to walk the bus students to the front of the school.

Fortunately, Annelise is among these. I grab her hand; bend over as we stride down the hall together at the head of the line.

"Annelise, what's going on?" Silence.

"I noticed you didn't line up to say good-bye."

"I didn't get a moment of science," she suddenly spits out.

Whoa! Where is this coming from? This has never happened before. I flash back to two days prior when I spotted the Moments of Science list, the only one I had not removed from the board. On impulse, I took it down, deciding to revisit and value each moment and deliver one more public service announcement for critical thinking skills.

"On September 14, Austin had a hypothesis about his snakeskin." I remember this well, but I wonder if Austin does, so I ask him.

"Yeah, I thought the snake was run over by a car while it was shedding." Austin *does* remember exactly what he said nine months ago.

I read a few more until I get to November 20 when "Nicole wondered why do leaves stay on bushes longer than on trees and she had a hypothesis about it." I don't remember this one so again I ask, "Nicole, do you remember your hypothesis?"

"Well, since trees are higher up, their leaves get blown off when it's windy, but the leaves on the bushes are lower and protected from the wind."

I am stunned at the pride and ownership each student feels for his or her moment. As I continue down the list, smiling broadly at each honoree, I receive a knowing look of recognition in return as each one remembers his or her contribution. Kyle remembers learning that layers of rock pile up and compress over time to form the streambed. Téo remembers comparing crayfish to bears and horses because they all raise up their front legs to defend themselves. We note that Emma wondered, "If bees became extinct, would flowers become extinct?" just weeks before the decline in bee populations and the resulting difficulty for farmers were front-page news. There I am, kvelling over the success of this classroom tradition while Annelise (and now I wonder how many others) is having it rubbed in her face one more time that she did not get to participate. Clearly she had been waiting her turn patiently and had expected to land in this club.

"Annelise, just because I didn't notice a moment of science doesn't mean you didn't have one," I explain, searching my brain for the right words as we rush toward the buses. Annelise keeps looking down, disappointment and indignation steaming off her back.

"Listen, why don't you call me this summer when you have a moment of science. Your mom is usually waiting for you after school. I'll give her . . ."

"She doesn't even know what they are," Annelise cuts me to the quick.

"Okay, then I will explain moments of science to her right now. Your mom knows my phone number so she can call me. I'd love to hear about your discoveries."

We have reached the front steps and Annelise's mom, Christina, is indeed waiting for her on the front lawn. Annelise herself is unmoved. I quickly tell Christina what's going on.

"Yes, I read about those in your newsletter," reports Christina. "It's when a student has a thinking question or observes something interesting, right?"

Christina suggests that Annelise could send me an e-mail. Great, we're all on the same page. I try one more time. Maybe I can bestow a special category of discovery right here on the school grounds. It's still the last day, right?

"Annelise, what did you do that you thought should be a moment of science?"

"I found the egg," shoots out with indignance. Wasn't it obvious?

She's referring to half of a tan eggshell that she shared recently with the class. Larger than a songbird's egg, we looked it up together in Harrison's *A Field Guide to Birds' Nests*, but it was too difficult to make a for-sure identification. Many students had brought in eggs, eggshells, nests built in paint buckets—none received moments of science. I am aware of the faculty lining up behind me for the group farewell, but I try one more time.

"Annelise can you tell me how you found the egg?" Maybe there was an unusual process that I overlooked.

Annelise sprints over to her mom; leans against her leg.

"You tell her!"

"No, Annelise. I want you to tell me."

A few seconds is all I have now. With a sigh, I turn to join my colleagues. We wave in unison as the buses pull out of the circle, then drive around one more time. I am wondering what I will say next if Annelise is still there when I turn around. She is not.

Over the next few days, I repeat this story to Ann, my friend and mentor and a retired master teacher, and to David, who had a similar experience with one of his ace AP Bio students. I ruminate on how to do it differently next year. The intent was never to ensure that every student "makes the board." It is true that from time to time, I am more tuned in to a struggling student, waiting for a moment to occur. I will also admit to trying to balance the gender on the list, but for the most part, moments are reserved for truly original thought.

Two weeks after that last day of school, I receive the following e-mail:

Hi Laurie guess what! I got five moments of science! The first one was when I was at a beach, and I found some baby sand-crabs, then I found a mole in my yard, then I was at a camp and found crayfish in a pond, then I saw a giant toad and my last moment of science was when I found a garden snake in my yard!!!!!! Signed, Annelise.

Relieved that I have not scarred Annelise for life, I make a note in my planning book to revise my introduction to moments of science the following year (the year Julius answered the turkey question). But after my careful explanation in the fall, I promptly forget all about moments of science *at home* until early April, when David and I have a long talk over dinner.

Today one of David's current students stopped in after school and said, "I guess I just don't think out of the box, since I've never earned a moment of science." I remind him of Annelise's story, and we ponder how to fix this unexpected dilemma of discouraged students who don't "make the list."

I make a sudden command decision to present each student with an official Moments of Science scroll at our poetry coffeehouse the following week. Most of the parents will be there, and I will encourage each family to post the scroll at home to remind everyone to ask thinking questions and observe the world with new eyes.

The next day at school I use 8½-by-14-inch copy paper, select two columns, type Moments of Science in a Lucida Blackletter font centered over each column, print, copy, and cut in half vertically. I roll up nineteen scrolls and tie them with red ribbon. After the poetry celebration, on the last day of school before our April vacation, I also print the following in my weekly newsletter:

I hope you will post the Moments of Science scroll where everyone in your family can see it. Try to catch your children asking thinking questions or making interesting observations. Maybe you will find yourself thinking like a scientist too! And please let me know what happens.

I wait for two days after we return from spring break. No one mentions a moment of science. I decide to ask.

"I'm really curious. Did anyone have a moment of science during vacation? Has anyone recorded their moments on the scroll?"

We go around the circle, and as usual, anyone can pass. Six students share their moments.

"Why are the flaps on the plane moving?"

"Why do so many robins come to my house?"

"I haven't written it down yet, but how come so many dark-eyed juncos come to my house?"

"Why can we see crayfish when there is still ice in the lake?"

"I found a creepy crawly with more than eight legs. What is it?"

"Wherever you dig up mud, there is water underneath."

Most of my students asked questions. I note the staying power of my first instruction at the stream—when you are out in the natural world, look around and ask a question. I was hoping for more, but this is a reasonable start. I am also pleased that there is only one copycat moment. My students are taking this seriously.

The next day I get my first unprompted report. Rachel tells me about her moment of science at home. "I found an insect with eight legs?" Rachel's confusion registers in her voice because she knows from our study that insects are supposed to have six legs. Andres, who overhears our conversation, explains that she found a spider, "also called an arachnid." Rachel and I go to our classroom library and find a book on spiders that she tucks into her reading folder.

Two weeks later, Luke's dad comes in for his weekly volunteer duty during math time. He sits down and announces, "I have a moment of science. I'm looking out the window, and I can see how much greener the woods are since the last time I was here." I want to go over and hug him.

A few days later Andres walks through the door and announces, "Laurie, I had a moment of science." I am thrilled that my students are finding their way as scientists. Slowly the momentum of noting personal moments of science is gaining.

"Fantastic, Andres, tell me about it."

Andres always tells his stories in a slow, measured way, his voice rising at the end of each sentence as he works out his ideas.

"Well, I was at my father's *friend's?* house and I saw something on the *ground?* and I went *over?* and I thought it was a *moth?* and it *was?* and Josh said to bring it over to a *table?* and I got to watch it drying its wings."

"High five, Andres! Thank you so much for telling me."

During lunch that day, I see Peter's father, Matt, and remember I have not yet responded to his offer to come and talk about some aspect of his job as a doctor. I approach Matt and tell him to go for whatever he thinks makes sense. When he suggests starting with the questions he asks himself, I flash a big smile.

"Perfect, show us how a doctor is like a scientist. Show us your moments of science."

❋   ❋   ❋

The following year is even better. When I explain moments of science at parent conferences in the fall, Cynthia immediately remembers her daughter Samantha's observation that the water level in her tea glass goes into "points." Denise remembers Sydney's recently asking a question about her world.

As soon as the first moment of science arises in the classroom, I create a special place on the chalkboard to record, display, and value moments of science at home. When we return to school in January I ask students to report on moments at home. Olivia's question—Where did the first seed come from?—soon elicits, Where did the first plant come from? The first animal?

"I think Olivia's question made you think of questions right *now*, which is fantastic. But remember how we "stop and think" while we are reading? You need to do the same thing out in the natural world. When you are outside, just stop for a moment and notice what you are wondering about."

I will continue to use moments of science to help me *teach* science. I have found a process that works not only for nature study but also for all the scientific content I am required to teach. My students and I will continue to learn factual information (insect body parts, life cycle stages, or forms of matter), but we will learn in an environment where observation, questioning, hypothesizing, looking for evidence, and drawing conclusions are a natural part of the learning process, where students begin to look around them with eyes wide open and trust their own thinking wherever they happen to be.

CHAPTER 3

A Year at the Stream—Autumn

In the next three chapters—covering autumn, winter, and spring—I take you to the little stream behind our school and show you what it looks and sounds like to take a class of twenty-one second graders outside to explore the natural world throughout a single year—on warm days in our shirtsleeves, on bitter cold days in full snow gear, on bright sunny days as well as gray rainy ones.

Following each visit to the stream I reflect on my students' experience that day and over time, make observations about individual students or group dynamics, and share thoughts about how to tweak our routines to afford more time for exploration, to strengthen critical thinking skills, or to encourage more thoughtful nature journaling. I sometimes incorporate vignettes from other years to expand on a particular reflection or to demonstrate a wider range of possibilities.

I also include entries from my personal nature journal to convey my own evolution as a naturalist and my attempts to practice the critical thinking that I will be asking of my students. Finally, there are samples of student journal entries collected over seven years of nature study, which illustrate a variety of student abilities.

September 9, Monday morning on the way to school

I am one block from the school parking lot when I see wild turkeys in the road. I immediately step on the brake and approach at five miles an hour. My first instinct is to count—there are twelve turkeys. Next I look for the longer, redder wattle of the males and conclude I'm looking at a flock of females. Five years ago I would have thought, "Wow, look at the turkeys," and moved on.

MONDAY, SEPTEMBER 21: GETTING READY

After school I head out to the stream site to prepare for our first day of stream study. I take a walk up the streambed (no water, no surprise) and discover that some kids have built a tipi along the stream over the summer. There have always been tipi structures in the woods that we admire, but this one is too close to the stream, and I decide it will be a distraction. It takes me about twenty minutes to dismantle it. I have to look carefully to find the topmost branches because they are cleverly intertwined and quite secure.

I throw the poles farther into the woods and turn toward locating a bit of poison ivy to show my students—not much this year, since it has been such a dry summer. I refresh my memory about how I divide up the territory—spreading three groups at different sites along the stream. I would love to stay longer, but I drag myself away to get to a teacher association meeting on time.

TUESDAY, SEPTEMBER 22: MEETING OUR STREAM

The early arrivals, walkers and students dropped off by car, are already in my classroom when Laura, a former student now in third grade, stops by to tell me that her class watched a monarch chrysalis hatch yesterday. Our paths do not cross very often because she is in a different wing of the school, and she has come out of her way to see me. Then Ana, now in fourth grade, arrives with a pinecone that she thought was neat because it was not opened yet. I spend a minute with each of them, ask a few questions, and thank them for sharing.

"What a perfect way for me to start the day. How did you know that today is our first day of stream study?"

The rest of my students arrive, hang up their jackets, throw lunch boxes into the bins, take down chairs, and walk over to the whiteboard to read my morning message.

"We will go to the stream after recess today. What do you think we will see? Write your ideas here." By the time the bell rings we have: fossils, water, salamanders, and leaves. As a class we add: grass, soil (originally offered as dirt), waves, bugs, frogs, fish, birds, caterpillars, fungus, logs, chipmunks, trash.

I am eager to get started. During story time I show the map that I drew in my nature journal of my very own first sit spot at the University of New Hampshire (see Figure 3.1). I point out all the details I included—water strider pool, raccoon tracks, sand bar, poison ivy vine, moss-covered root, boulders, New York ferns, and a sampling of identified trees—sugar maple, eastern hemlock, white pine and white oak.

I soon launch into my discussion of the three outdoor hazards, but there is only enough time to introduce poison ivy before going to music class. I assure my students we will continue after recess, but Sydney wants to know now, "What are the other two?" When I answer, "Bees and wasps and deer ticks,"

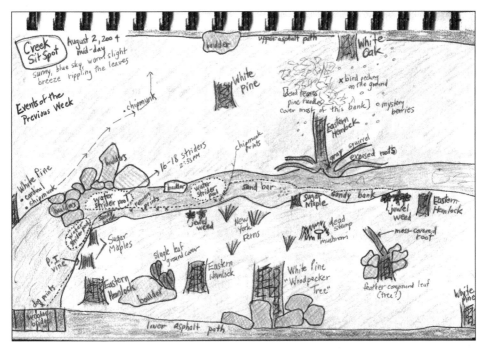

FIGURE 3.1 - I drew this map of my creek sit spot in my very first nature journal.

Leslie becomes very nervous about the possibility of bees. She was stung over the summer and is already anxious about the bees swarming on the playground.

"I'm not trying to scare you, Leslie," I assure her. "I want you to feel strong. I want you to know what to look for so you can avoid bees and *not* get stung." (See Chapter 1, Tip #4.)

By the time my students return from recess, Leslie seems willing to give it a try. I review the safety precautions for bees and wasps and deer ticks and then switch gears by asking why we will need to be quiet when we go out into the woods.

"So that we don't scare the animals away."

"Animals are quiet in the woods too, why?"

"So they can find food to eat, a fox, for example, might want to eat a deer," says Daniel.

Together we also establish the idea that animals are quiet so they do not become *another* animal's food, or prey.

At this point I demonstrate fox walk, owl eyes, and deer ears, ideas developed by the Kamana Naturalist Training Program. I step into the circle of students sitting on the rug, and, simulating a fox, I walk on the outer edges of my feet (to better feel the bumps, holes, and sticks on the ground and avoid making too much noise) and look straight ahead (to slow me down). I cup my hands over my ears, moving them from side to side to simulate deer ears, and I open my eyes wide like an owl. When I ask for volunteers to demonstrate, hands fly up eagerly. (Another day I will explain how an owl uses peripheral vision. My students will stand with arms outstretched and try to see their wiggling fingers without moving their eyes.)

Chase crouches way down, bends his knees, and fox-walks gracefully across the carpeting, owl eyes bright. We are ready!

I assign stream groups to parents and identify tables in the room that will be their headquarters for the rest of the year. I call each group of children to fox-walk over to their tables where they will record the date and weather in their journals. Seven pairs of legs bent at the knee and feet turned to walk on the outside edges of sneakers—move seriously across the floor. It is a beautiful sight and an auspicious beginning for nature study.

My students are excited to be going out. During indoor recess they worried that stream study would be cancelled because of the rain. I pass out my collection of donated plastic rain ponchos for protection against the drizzle; we progress down the hall, nature journals in hand, until we reach the back door. As soon as we step outside onto the grass, we begin our fox walk. It is absolutely magical to look back and see a line of fox-walking children and adults. We walk in silence behind the school except for the soft crunching beneath our feet, which soon prompts me to stop in front of a section of lawn covered with twigs, bundles of dry fallen leaves, and hundreds of acorns.

"When you see something in the natural world, you can always ask a question," I begin. "What do you think happened here? Where did all of these leaves, twigs, branches, and acorns come from?"

"Wind, wind, wind," my students chorus and indeed, a major windstorm passed through two days prior, the edge of Hurricane Ike, which was centered in Texas.

We enter the woods and follow the dry streambed together all the way to the poison ivy patch. There we gather around and confirm everything I pointed out in the morning—the leaves of three, the longer stem of the central leaf, the varying leaf shapes.

We continue up the streambed, wet with puddles here and there, visiting each group's sit spot. I explain that when there is more water it will flow across these flat rock formations.

"Okay, everyone back to your sit spots and start exploring. Find at least one plant or animal that you would like to observe carefully and draw."

Students are on the ground, lifting up leaves and rocks, digging in the moist soil on the stream banks (see Figure 3.2). They find salamanders, slugs, moths, leaves, bone, bark, acorns, and fossil rocks. After fifteen minutes it starts to rain harder and we reluctantly head back inside, taking a sampling of our finds with us but leaving the live specimens behind.

Wet ponchos piled in a heap, we sit down to take a quick look at our predictions on the whiteboard. We erase what we did *not* find: fish, frogs, and waves. I change "water" to "puddles." To "leaves" I add, "mostly on the trees, some on the ground." I also add "slugs, moths, bone, bark, acorns," and "lots of rocks."

For the next twenty-five minutes everyone is engaged, drawing in nature journals. Crayons and colored pencils share space across the tables with leaves, bark, acorns, and rocks. My students are eager to use color because during writing workshop, when they plan their stories, they may only use pencil to make

FIGURE 3.2 - Students search for salamanders and insects at their sit spot.

their quick sketches. Everyone draws more than one object. Some use more than one page; some draw small enough to fit several illustrations on one page; some add labels. Luis, a talented artist, after placing a detailed drawing in each corner of the page—bone, leaf, acorn, and salamander and pinecone—lightly shades in a blue and green background (see Figure 3.3).

We have just enough time before the dismissal bell rings to gather back in the circle, where I ask students to share their entries with one person sitting next to them (see Figure 3.4).

After school I start a new piece of chart paper titled "Stream Study Observations." Under "September," I make a permanent list of our observations to revisit before we go out next week. We will add to this chart throughout the year for each month, comparing and contrasting as we go (see Figure 3.5).

Reflections

A combination of weather, the group dynamics and prior knowledge of my students, the skill and comfort level of parent volunteers, and my own experi-

FIGURE 3.3 - Luis uses detail in his drawings and records the weather in both words and pictures— rainy and overcast.

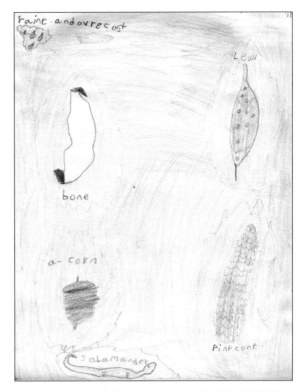

FIGURE 3.4 (BELOW) - Sharing nature journals affirms their value and provides models for future entries.

FIGURE 3.5 - The list of September observations is our longest. In October we start to record the changes we have noted.

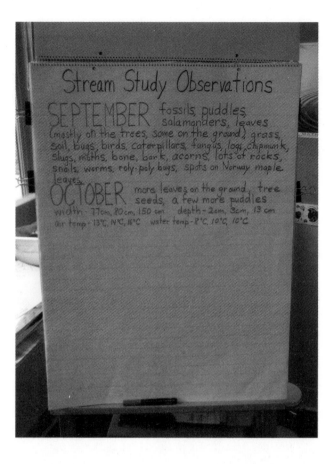

ence as a naturalist influence my decisions about how to start off each year. For example, I was not planning to stop in front of the fallen acorns, but as I become more and more attuned to the natural world, I try to turn my own impromptu observations and questions into teachable moments for my students.

As teachers we also continue to improve and fine-tune our practice each year. In the early years of nature study, I encouraged my young naturalists to write and draw their observations sitting or standing next to the stream. But over time I noticed that, enticed by the natural world, many completed their entries as quickly as possible and asked, "Can I play now?" Rather than coax or cajole, thanks to this particular rainy day, I discovered quite by accident that coming away from the stream site was an effective strategy for supporting second graders as nature journalists. When we returned to the classroom, we became a group of writers just as we do during our daily writing workshop. A focused energy filled the room, and the overall quality of these initial entries improved dramatically.

I also learned this year that heavy rain and nature journals are a disastrous mix. Three students returned with soggy front covers in their hands, pulled right out of their metal ring bindings. Although I managed to cobble their journals together with clear packaging tape, I took it as another good reason to leave our journals inside.

On the other hand I integrate many of the same teaching points from year to year. On the first day I try to express my wonder and respect for the natural world as often as possible:

"Be sure to put that rock back just the way you found it. Underneath is a home for many small animals."

"Shh, everyone listen. Do you hear that birdsong? Isn't that beautiful?"

I also highlight the students who are already avid nature lovers:

"CJ, can you tell us how you know where to find salamanders?"

"Look how carefully Megan holds the salamander so it won't get hurt."

Finally, I set aside student journals with detailed observational drawings, labels, effective use of color, thoughtful comments, or questions. I will present these journals as models to inspire other students before we go out the following week.

Saturday, September 13, Lodi, NY, Bike Ride

I rarely go for a bike ride without the harness of my Nikon Monarch binoculars firmly in place across my chest. I am guessing that serious bikers would not put up with my frequent bird-watching stops nor would serious birders be interested in the common species I encounter, but David puts up with me and so biking and birding have become synonymous for us.

The red-tailed hawks are everywhere today—on the electric wires, up in the trees. They fly away as we approach on our bicycles, but they do not go too far and land one electric pole ahead of us. Each time I am able to make out the russet color on their tails. I am finally ready to trust that whenever I see a hawk of this size in our rural neighborhood, it is most likely a red-tailed.

We pass a muddy plowed field and hear plaintive squealing—a flock of killdeer. David points out the small pond on the opposite side of the road, a resting spot for six female mallards, and a good water supply for the killdeer. Once again David models his scientific thinking for me. It doesn't automatically occur to me to ask myself, "Why are there killdeer in this particular field?" I must remember to incorporate this kind of thinking for my students. "If you see an animal or plant, ask yourself, why might it be here?"

TUESDAY, SEPTEMBER 29: ASKING QUESTIONS

Ninety percent chance of rain according to the forecast. At a quarter to twelve it starts raining so we have indoor recess . . . again. I go back to the classroom and start scrambling to make another plan for the afternoon, but by twelve ten, when the three stream-study parents arrive, the skies clear and we are back in stream business. Five minutes later, my class is gathered on the rug looking at our observations from last week and making some predictions about what will change. After a week of rain, the general consensus is more water, flowing water, deeper water.

Today I introduce a new tool—the hand lens. I open up to the page in *Crawdad Creek* by Scott Russell Sanders where Elizabeth and her brother, Michael, use a hand lens to take a closer look at a dragonfly. (See Chapter 1, Tip #7.)

"If you want to see detail like this, a hand lens is a great tool to take out into the natural world," I explain in a hushed voice.

I also invite my students to ask a question today about something they see or wonder about at the stream and I tell my water strider story.

One day I am watching water striders. They seem to stay in one spot as they float downstream a bit and then kick to get themselves back upstream again. Each kick creates a wonderful circle of rippled water. I watch their four legs for a long time, but they move so fast that no matter how hard I stare, I cannot figure out what they are doing. "How do they move?" I wonder.

I am just about to leave when sunlight suddenly peeks through the trees making shadows on the bottom of the creek bed. I quickly realize that I am looking at the shadow of a water strider and it's like I'm looking through a microscope. Now I can see that the front legs pull back like the oars of a rowboat! I am very excited by my discovery and so pleased that I stayed just a little longer that day. And if I hadn't asked the question, "How do they move?" I never would have noticed.

I then reveal that it is only several days later when, searching for a water strider image online, I realize that they are insects.

"How many legs does an insect have?" I ask my class and they spontaneously shout out, "Six."

"You're right. Water striders have *six* legs, not four, and it was the *middle* ones doing the rowing. What I thought were antennae dimpling the water were actually their front legs. I have been fooled many times in the natural world. I am learning to look very carefully and then look some more. Now let's watch the Red group fox-walk to their stream table to write the date and weather on their next page."

All seven students are experts. Then one at a time, the remaining two groups fox-walk, prepare their journals, and line up at the door, hand lenses dangling from their necks on bright red thread. This week each group receives collection equipment as well: clear plastic tanks for live creatures and bug magnifiers for dead plants or animals (see Figure 3.6). The live creatures usually stay at the

FIGURE 3.6 - Students wear hand lenses and carry a collection tank at the stream.

stream but the others can return to the classroom. Before we step out into the hall, I remind them of their focus today.

"Remember, while you're exploring, notice what questions are popping into your mind. You will write them down in your nature journals when we return."

We stay out for about thirty-five minutes. One group finds salamanders. My group finds slugs, snails, worms, roly-poly bugs, and lots of leaves—everyone notices the big black spots on the Norway maple leaves. The collection tanks come in handy for observing the live animals with a minimum of handling.

We bring a collection back to the classroom where we first gather in the circle to hear four or five questions. I want to provide a model for those students who may have returned without any questions in mind.

"When you go to your tables, write down your questions and then you may draw one or more of the finds we brought back. Remember that this is obser-vational drawing—draw exactly what you see, not what you imagine."

Some students bring questions directly from their explorations at the stream. Others only figure out their questions as they are drawing. Eighteen out of twenty (one student is absent) students have questions that fall into several categories.

Questions of origin: how did the spiders get there, how did the worm get to the stream, how did the hole get under the tree, where did the black spots come from on the leaves, where did the rocks come from, where did the water come from, how do mushrooms get on trees, and while we're at it, where do all the animals in the world come from?

Specific animal questions: do salamanders come out of eggs, why are salamanders slimy, why do they stink, how do they squiggle, how does a salamander walk in the deep water (I've never seen it), how do snails drink? I wonder what kind of animal these eggs come from?

Physical questions: I wonder if the stream goes around in a circle. When you pick up a rock, why does the water turn brown and cloudy? Why did the rock split? How did the pattern on the wood get there? Did it already have it when it was growing or did it have something to do with the water? (See Figure 3.7.)

FIGURE 3.7 - Samantha tries to answer her own questions as she ponders the pattern in the wood.

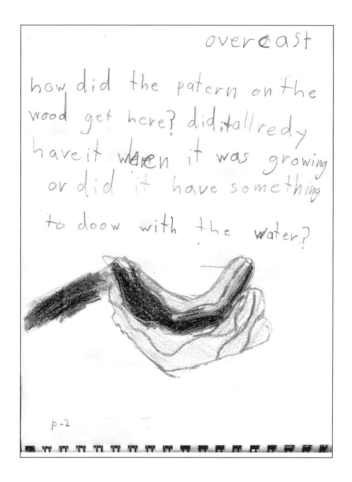

While students complete their journal entries, Karen, a parent volunteer who is also a veterinarian, helps one of my special education students. Karen shows her how you can look at the underside of a salamander by holding up and looking through the bottom of the collection tank. (Today I bend the rules and bring back a live salamander because Jocelyn, not always an engaged student, is absolutely gripped by nature study and this particular creature.) When Jocelyn notices something red on the salamander, Karen identifies it immediately as the salamander's heart. Before we leave today, every student has a chance to see the heart beating through the skin.

Reflections

I learn something new with each outdoor visit and this time because of a very knowledgeable parent. Last week Karen identified the northern two-line salamanders we were finding, and now we can clearly see the two dark lines running down the sides of Jocelyn's specimen. I am keenly aware that, although I will be sharing the beating salamander heart with my future students, my previous classes never had this opportunity. As a classroom teacher I am a generalist. I do not have the training of an ecologist, biologist, or conservationist so I am extremely grateful when a parent like Karen agrees to volunteer. Still, I believe that my enthusiasm in learning alongside my students is a powerful teaching tool. Former students like Ana and Laura, who identify me with their own love of the natural world, renew my confidence and reassure me that I do not need to know everything.

There are so many routines to establish at the beginning of the school year. Nature study is no exception. I try to introduce only one new routine each week and revisit the others, in this case observational drawing. But in fact other teaching points emerge, and I try to space them out as best I can.

Before I send my students off with their journals, I hold one up to demonstrate how to find their last entry. I train them to avoid skipping pages and to use both sides of each sheet of paper.

I also try to include as much sharing as possible to value the work they have been assigned. I am always mindful of time constraints. There are days for partner shares, sharing in small groups, and individual sharing around the circle, or today's version, when only a few individuals share with the whole class.

September 26, Lodi Woods

Out in the meadow, I begin noticing ash trees because their leaves are the same colors as the ash growing near the house—mustard and claret. First one tree, then a cluster appears. Soon I am picking them out in the landscape and along the path. David told me that thirty years ago, the word was to cut down all of your ash trees because a disease was spreading. He never did and now he has many ash trees that may yet be attacked by the emerald ash borer, now making its way through New York.

TUESDAY, OCTOBER 6: COLLECTING EVIDENCE AND USING FIELD GUIDES

I receive an e-mail in the morning from Jean, our tree expert, who tells me that next week will be the best time for her to visit. I immediately start rethinking our day at the stream. I was planning to review the questions my students wrote down in their nature journals last week. One question, "Where did the water come from?" would be answered by reading *Where the River Begins* by Thomas Locker. Instead I read *Meeting Trees* by Scott Russell Sanders in preparation for Jean's visit. In the afternoon I continue Sanders' theme of trees as friends and tell my goldenrain tree story. (See Chapter 1, Tip #6.)

- -

Yesterday a friend brought me some seedpods. I took one look at them and recognized an old friend. Let me tell you how we met.

One warm day in the middle of July, I met a tree draped with yellow flower clusters radiant in the summer sun. I wanted to know my new friend's name, but I could not find it in any tree field guide. (All eyes are on me in that delicious moment when I know my students are entranced by a story.) The tree happened to be on a college campus in New Hampshire so I called Plant Maintenance (that's the office that takes care of all the trees, grass, and plants on campus) and the Horticulture Department (that's where students learn all about plants).

The next day I had a message from a professor in the horticulture department. It turned out my special tree has two names. The Latin name is Koelreuteria paniculata *(cole-roo-tare-y-uh pah-nick-you-lah-tah), but people commonly call it the goldenrain tree. I visited this magnificent tree every day and watched the green, lantern-shaped seedpods develop over time.*

A year later biking around Ithaca I started noticing goldenrain trees in bloom on the city sidewalks. So when my friend Laura presented me with five pale-green, lantern-shaped seedpods, I shouted, "Koelreuteria paniculata" and felt like an old friend had come to visit.

- -

As we prepare to go outside, again *without* our journals, Daniel insists, "But it's a beautiful day!" so I change plans again and give the following directions:

FIGURE 3.8 - Students examine the bark of a tree as they draw in their nature journals.

"Meet at least four trees at your secret sit spot today, collect leaves for each tree, draw the texture of the bark in your nature journals (I show different texture possibilities on the whiteboard), and then you can explore."

On the path into the woods Samantha picks up a cluster of pine needles.

"How many needles, how many needles?" Daniel is almost jumping up and down.

Together we count five out loud.

"I know, I know," yells Helena, trying to remember what we learned in Sanders' book this morning. "It's the white oak!"

"It's definitely white but not oak," I coach.

"White *pine,*" Helena concludes triumphantly.

We look up to find the white pine tree and then wait for the rest of the class to join us in our discovery.

We move on, and I stop at a pile of beads on the edge of the path. Two weeks ago on the way back to our classroom I mistook them for berries. I was very excited because I thought we would be able to use them to identify the cherry trees in our woods. The beads were brown and green and orange and, without my glasses, I thought I was looking at berries that had dropped over time—green and orange ones composting into brown. Then last week when I pointed them out to my stream group, Sydney walking past, unflappable, declared "beads." They were plastic. This time I tell my story and end with the moral, "When you are out in the natural world you need to be a very careful observer or you may be fooled like I was."

Now each group heads to its stream site, and we start looking for trees. Today it is difficult to keep my group focused because the stream itself is so alluring. But eventually we choose four trees to show to our tree expert. Daniel goes off on his own to start drawing a tree, and soon everyone else is working in their journals (see Figure 3.8).

I work with Nicholas, a special education student who is carefully drawing the white oak, the biggest tree at our site. He shades in a trunk and branches with his pencil. I encourage him to add the detail of the bark and he does. Then we see another branch sticking out with leaves on it. Nicholas agrees that this is the "roller coaster" leaf mentioned in Sanders's book, and I celebrate his finding a white oak.

Kaitlyn chooses a tree with reddish-brown bark, and Helena chooses the Norway maple. The leaves of Jocelyn's tree are too high to gather, but they are easily recognizable—yellow with seven leaflets. I carefully draw leaf and bark for each tree so that I can keep the different species straight in my own mind.

When everyone finishes drawing we head inside, but not before Daniel shouts out, "I found one of our salamander friends!" We gather around to admire before returning it to the stream habitat. Taking the journals outside today worked like a charm—everyone returns with multiple drawings of bark (see Figure 3.9).

Jocelyn carries a hefty piece of bark and also the most minute hair, which she believes to be from a raccoon. She also finds extremely tiny leaves, and I praise her for being such a careful observer.

Back in the classroom each group presses its leaves between dictionary pages and uses field guides for the first time, with some impressive success. Away from the stream, my group is exceptionally focused. Excited to recognize the tulip flower we saw in the Sanders book, Helena continues looking and finds the white pine needles next. Kaitlyn finds oak leaves in her field guide and wonders whether they are white oak. We keep looking together until we satisfy ourselves that we have both red and white oak leaves on our table. Daniel and his mom, Karen, work on identifying a horse chestnut leaf with five leaflets. We then turn our attention to our seeds, as we have some that are definitely not acorns. Just as we are about to clean up, Jocelyn calls me over excitedly to a little pile of soil on the table.

"Laurie, look what I have—dirt."

"Where did you find that?" I ask.

Jocelyn shows me how she stuck her finger inside the hollow cylindrical piece of bark and scraped along the inside of the bark to collect the soil.

"You have just earned a moment of science," I exclaim with a broad smile. "You discovered compost."

I grab a clear plastic display box and put the compost inside. We have only a few minutes to gather on the rug before it is time to go home. I announce that Jocelyn earned a moment of science. I hold up the bark and ask what used to be inside of it.

After a few possibilities Eric offers, "Wood. Wood from a tree."

"Yes, I think you are right. This piece of bark used to be part of a tree. All of the wood inside started to decompose and turned into this beautiful soil that we call compost. You know all of the stuff we collect for compost every day—apple cores, banana peels, paper towels? It goes into a huge composting container, starts to heat up and change, or what scientists call *decompose*. Slowly, over time, it turns into this soil called *compost*."

Jocelyn has a few minutes to explain how she found the compost before I glance up at the clock and send my students off to line up for dismissal.

Reflections

As I prepared to share Jocelyn's moment of science, it occurred to me that most of my students (unless they have their own gardens at home) have no experience with compost. They do not understand that what we collect for

FIGURE 3.9 - Samantha draws the bark of a shagbark hickory and adds deer "scrape," deer scat, and lichen "growing on tree."

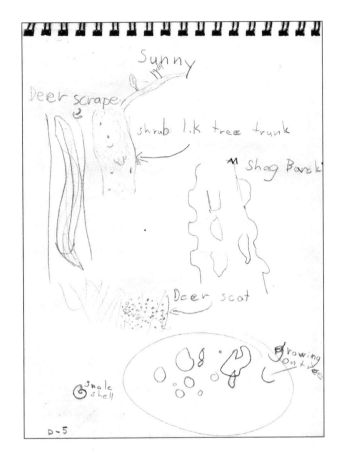

compost—food scraps, compostable brown paper towels, wooden ice cream sticks, and so on—is only the beginning of a long process. This became a perfect teachable moment to make that connection. I find that nature study not only offers these teachable moments related to our daily lives but also to the content of our science curriculum.

Nicholas and Jocelyn receive daily special education services this year both inside and outside the classroom. They look forward to stream study each week, and I am thrilled and intrigued by how engaged and alive they become once we step outside.

I think about Jonathan, a former student diagnosed with ADHD (attention-deficit hyperactivity disorder) who also came alive during stream study. Jonathan struggled to focus whenever he had to put pencil to paper. During

FIGURE 3.10 -

Remembering her moment of science, Sophie lists "tree trunks" along with rocks and roots next to a gray dot.

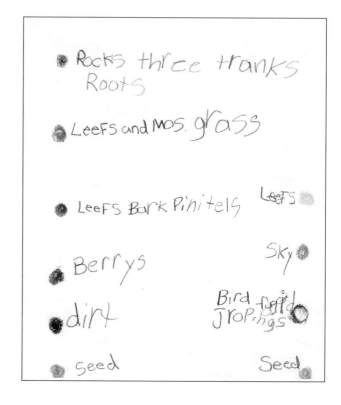

writing workshop, he would sit quietly, staring at his unopened folder unless I sat down, quickly reviewed his next writing steps, and continued to check in every five minutes.

He also had difficulty listening to stories, with or without illustrations. One afternoon in early October our school occupational therapist, Jill, joined us during story time to observe Jonathan. When I noticed him at the back edge of the crowd talking to Luke, I immediately reminded him to come and sit in front of me. The rest of my class was spellbound, gripped by the ongoing drama of *Gooseberry Park* by Cynthia Rylant, a favorite every year. I made eye contact with Jonathan frequently to keep his attention, but he moved his head slowly from left to right and back again throughout the entire story.

While my students ate lunch in the cafeteria, Jill and I had a quick consult. She told me about creating a "sensory diet" for Jonathan—some kind of activity that he could use during a half-hour work session to calm himself, like sitting down on the floor and pushing his legs against a wall. I suggested that I continue to observe Jonathan, and we agreed on a meeting time the following week to plan a strategy.

That same day we happened to have stream study with a focus on seeing colors. As a class, we brainstormed a list of the most common colors in the natural world—green (for trees, leaves, and grass), brown (for trees and soil), gray (for rocks)—and a few others—yellow, red, orange, white, blue, and black. We prepared our nature journals with little dots of color spread out across the page. Outside, each group worked together, finding plants and animals of different colors and recording them next to the appropriate colors in the journals (see Figure 3.10). Lichen was particularly exciting that day—we found orange, yellow, white, and brown with white edges.

Jonathan loved this activity. He talked nonstop, shared his discoveries, and eagerly wrote down everything we found. He actually wrote more than anyone else in my group and stayed focused for the entire forty-five minutes at the stream.

"Look how much I wrote, Laurie," he declared, proudly showing me his work.

The following week Jonathan became fascinated with the measuring tape. After he completed his assigned task—measuring the width of a puddle with Erin—he proceeded to measure two logs and wandered up and down the stream working with the tape for the rest of our stream time. I could not help but ponder the contrast between Jonathan's ongoing engagement at the stream and his passive performance that morning.

In March I came across Jonathan staring out the window during activity time. I asked him if he would like to make a choice today and he said, "I'm watching the squirrels and their behaviors." He had noticed that one squirrel chased another one and it was up in a tree. One squirrel was eating the sunflower seeds on the ground under the feeder. I stood next to him a while and shared my observation of how the squirrel stands up on its hind legs to eat.

"Do you see how they hold their food, Jonathan? With their front paws?"

Five minutes later, Jonathan came to tell me that the paws "are like cups."

These students make me think about the research cited by Richard Louv in his book, *Last Child in the Woods: Saving Our Children from Nature-Deficit Disorder*. Louv cites several studies where "activities in natural, green settings were far more likely to leave ADD [ADHD] children better able to focus, concentrate" (2005, 106). Even studying or playing in rooms with a view of nature seemed to have a beneficial effect—especially for girls ages six to nine—on school performance, handling peer pressure, and avoiding problem behaviors. My experiences with Nicholas, Jocelyn, and Jonathan add anecdotal evidence to this growing body of data.

October 12, Lodi Woods

I finally start my walk at 4:00 p.m., which turns out to be the only time the sun comes out and stays a while. As I enter the woods, I hear a tree whining, scraping against a dead tree fallen alongside it. I walk down close to the creek, close my eyes listening to the trickle of water, the whining tree, and the elusive pecking of a woodpecker.

Later, when I come out on the access road, I am puzzled, frowning, wondering what hurricane blew through here. I walk a few minutes before realizing that a road crew has come through and hacked away at the young trees growing at the edge of the road. Six to eight feet high, the slender tree trunks stretch out their scraggly remains, so many upside-down straw brooms, as if a giant monster came through with long, sharp fingernails scratching through the trees.

At the end of the road, sits the perpetrator—a heavy piece of road equipment, its steel parts coated thickly with mud. Enormous, unyielding metal. All in stark contrast to the gentle contours of the trees I have been drinking in—horse chestnut, shagbark hickory, sugar maple, red maple, white oak, and white pine.

TUESDAY, OCTOBER 13: MEETING TREES

In the morning I finish reading *Crinkleroot's Guide to Knowing the Trees* by Jim Arnosky to the class. The last page is a perfect segue to our stream study today. Crinkleroot, a friendly woodland gnome, suggests that if we go out into the woods to meet trees we just might become experts like him.

This year our tree expert is Jean Elaine Grace, another Cornell University Department of Horticulture graduate student. She arrives laden with an array of twigs, leaves, and fruits, including shagbark hickory nuts, dogwood and sumac fruits, and delightfully scented twigs of spicy sassafras. After lunch she shares her collection with my students, teaching the difference between deciduous and evergreen trees and pointing out the leaf features to look for—simple versus compound, alternate versus opposite, smooth versus bumpy surface, smooth versus jagged edge (see Figure 3.11).

I show examples of leaf drawings in my nature journal, pass out balls of yarn, and explain that Jean will meet with each group for about fifteen minutes at their stream sites. Today we will need our journals outside again as we practice observational drawing.

"While you are waiting for Jean, mark the trees you want to meet by tying yarn around the trunks and draw the leaves of each."

The students in my group run to the trees they picked out last week. Helena spontaneously throws her arms around the trunk of "her" Norway maple. Jean

FIGURE 3.11 - Jean Grace shares her collection of compound and simple leaves.

FIGURE 3.12 - Jean Grace points out the features that confirm our tree is a pignut hickory.

follows close behind with her binoculars so that she can look high up into the trees to identify the leaves.

We find out that Kaitlyn's tree is a cherry, Jocelyn's an ash. We have a few extra minutes so I walk over to what I assume is a shagbark hickory. Jean points out that the smaller leaves make it a *pignut* hickory. When we find a nut on the ground, Jean again confirms pignut because of its relatively thin shell (see Figure 3.12).

When Jean leaves our group, we line up the leaves from each of our trees on a fallen log that we often use as a bench. Using the leaves as models, my students draw tiny leaves, some with no detail, some perfect replicas, and everything in between (see Figure 3.13).

Back in the classroom, we report on our new tree friends. Every group had a cherry, maple, and white oak. (See Chapter 1, Tip #6.)

Reflections

Jean is an excellent presenter. She talks rapidly, but her collection of fresh leaf samples and her infectious enthusiasm hold my students' attention. My goal today is an introduction to tree identification, not mastery. More important, I want my students to cultivate a growing love and appreciation for nature's largest plants.

Jean stays after dismissal to help me review the trees we identified. After six years of doing stream study, I am still trying to remember how to distinguish among the younger, more similar-looking trees. Each year I learn something new.

FIGURE 3.13 - A student records the purpose of Jean Grace's visit.

This year, in addition to the pignut hickory, I meet a linden tree, and for the first time, I understand how to identify an ash with compound opposite leaves. We review the acronym MADCAT HORSE that makes it easy to remember the only northern trees with opposite leaves—maple, ash, dogwood, catalpa, and horse chestnut.

When Jean leaves, I review the journals of the other two groups and find that the pages in a few are totally blank. But for the most part, my students have tried their best to make representational leaf drawings. I find myself questioning an earlier resolve to leave the nature journals inside. For the last two weeks, it has been a delight to watch my students leaning against trees, craning their necks to determine the shape of the crowns, journals in hand, writing and drawing. Perhaps specific assignments like drawing leaves and bark work better on site, while writing open-ended observations might be more suited to the classroom. I will continue to experiment and alternate between these two models throughout the year.

October 25, Lodi Woods

Bright yellow and orange leaves against a royal blue sky . . . As I turn back toward home, two flickers side by side, almost on top of each other on a tree trunk. Not my usual sighting on the ground. In the shade of the woods they look chocolate brown. Spotted breast, black moustache, red crescent on the back of the head, all easily visible. Only the black crescent on the breast is hidden from view. The sun on the fall leaves is glorious. Filled with the majesty of the three maple trees in our backyard, yellow leaves dazzling me, I honor the gift of my country home.

TUESDAY, OCTOBER 20: MEASUREMENT

On Monday after school I check the stream for running water. There are still only puddles, but I decide to go ahead with our first measurements, as we will need a baseline for the rest of the year. I plan to have our first discussion in the morning and prepare a measurement chart to fill in as we brainstorm ideas.

"When scientists make observations, they want to see how things change over time. One way they find evidence for change is by using measurements. What do you think we could measure to find out how our stream changes throughout the seasons?"

"We could do the same tests that we do in the trout tank," suggests Daniel.

"Perfect, we can measure how healthy our stream is," I affirm. "What else?"

Not surprisingly we do not get to the water right away. After all, we have not had much yet!

"We could measure how cold it is," Samantha adds tentatively.

"Yes. What gets cold outside?"

"Air," a few students shout out.

Eventually, as we consider how to measure water, our chart fills up quickly with different kinds of measurements, the tools we will need, and the units of measure. We list *width* (of the flowing stream or just puddles), how *tall* the water is (which I change to *depth)*, and together we substitute *temperature* for how hot or cold. When feet and inches come up for measuring depth, I introduce the metric system.

"In our country we measure with inches and feet and yards. It's called the United States Customary System. But all the other countries in the world and all scientists use the metric system. When we go outside to take measurements and observe how our stream changes over time, we will be scientists and use the metric system. We will use centimeters and meters to measure width and depth, and when we measure the temperature we will use the Celsius scale."

MEASUREMENT	TOOL	UNIT
Health	Chemical Indicators	Milligrams per Liter
Temperature	Thermometer	Degrees Celsius
Depth	Meter Stick	Centimeters
Width	Tape Measure	Centimeters
Speed	Timer, Meter Stick	Seconds per meter

After recess I use our measurement chart as a reference and point out the metric scale on each measuring tool. With my students' help, I review how to measure *width* with the measuring tape, *depth* with the meter stick. I draw a large thermometer on the whiteboard, and we examine the pattern of numbers—2, 4, 6, 8, 10—and conclude that each line on the scale stands for two degrees. My students will practice and hone these measurement skills throughout the year. They will be responsible for using a different tool each time and, when necessary, receive individual instruction and support from the adult in charge. I save *speed* for our November stream study when, hopefully, there will be enough water to get a measurement, and I turn to presenting the charts we will use for recording our data. (See the "Reflections" section that follows for more detail.)

"What is data?" I ask.

"We collected weather data at the end of September," remembers Shaundra.

"Yes, data is information, and it usually includes numbers. Our monthly measurements at the stream will be the data for this chart."

We meet in stream groups to prepare our journals and choose measurement jobs, which will rotate each month. We cut out the yearlong data charts and paste them on the inside back covers of our journals with glue stick (see Figure 3.14).

The three-ring circus begins as soon as we arrive at our stream sites. Tools in hand, my students sprint into action. Nicholas and Daniel position themselves on either side of the stream and stretch out the measuring tape across the largest puddle (see Figure 3.15). Mia and Jocelyn, holding thermometers, one in

Measurement	Oct	Nov	Dec	Jan	Feb	Mar	Apr	May
Width of Stream (cm=centimeters)								
Depth of Deepest Pool (cm=centimeters)								
Speed Sec= seconds per meter								
Air Temperature (°C= degrees Celsius)								
Water Temperature (°C= degrees Celsius)								

FIGURE 3.14 - Photocopies of the measurement chart are glued into the back cover of student nature journals.

FIGURE 3.15 - Students measure the width of the stream with the retractable measuring tape.

the air, one in the water, start counting to one hundred. Helena dips the meter stick into several puddles to find the deepest one. And I run around as fast as I can, making sure the thermometers are held on the top, not near the sensitive glass bulb, correcting the angle of the meter stick, helping my students read the confusing numbers on the tape measure, directing Victoria and Kaitlyn, who have no measuring job today, toward focused exploration.

As measurements are completed, I assist each student in recording his or her own data in the appropriate box with a unit of measure. Before we leave the stream, we sit down on our log (depending on time or weather, this may happen back in the classroom), where students report to one another until everyone

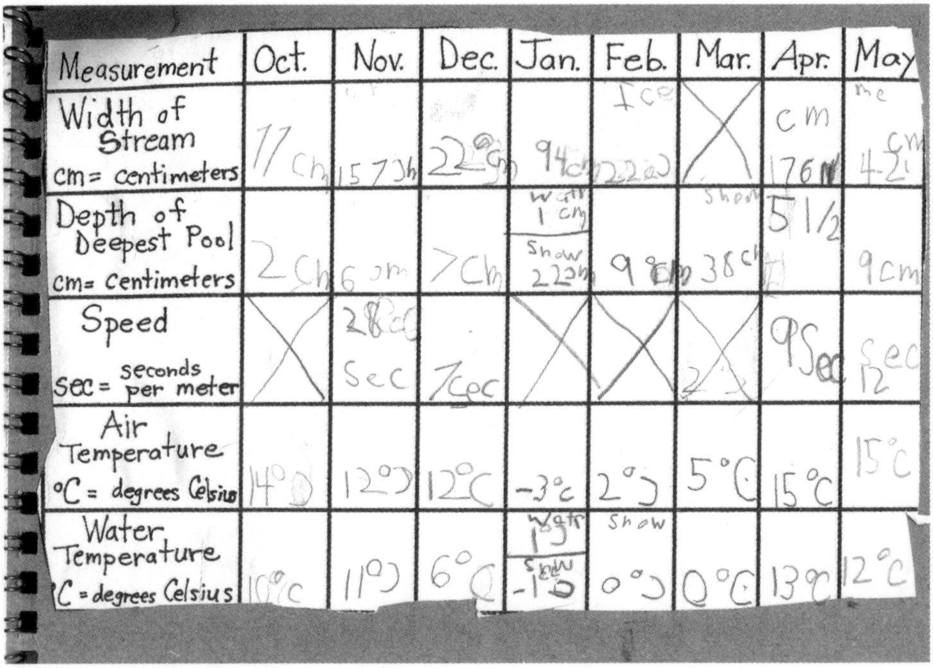

Measurement	Oct.	Nov.	Dec.	Jan.	Feb.	Mar.	Apr.	May
Width of Stream cm = centimeters	17 cm	15 7 Jh	22 cm	94 cm	Ice 22 cm	X	cm 176 m	me 42 cm
Depth of Deepest Pool cm = centimeters	2 cm	6 Jm	>cm	Snow 22 cm	wall 1 cm / 9 cm	Snow 38 cm	5 1/2	9 cm
Speed sec = seconds per meter	X	28 cm Sec	7 sec	X	X	2 X	9 Sec	sec 12
Air Temperature °C = degrees Celsius	14°	12°	12°C	−3°c	2°	5°C	15°C	15°C
Water Temperature C = degrees Celsius	10°c	11°	6°	watr / snow −1°	Snow 0°	0°C	13°	12°C

FIGURE 3.16 - Unit abbreviations are used for all recorded measurements.

has all measurements recorded. I demonstrate how to draw a big *X* in the box for speed since we have no measurement today (see Figure 3.16).

Back in the classroom, we compare the data from all three groups. We determine that the Blue group has the most water because their puddles are the widest and deepest—they report a thirteen-centimeter depth compared to two and three centimeters for the Red and Green groups.

We have about ten minutes to write and draw in our journals; again, the entries are more thoughtful when my students record together under my guidance (see Figure 3.17).

Reflections

I take time each year to present the measurement tasks, using the following teaching points:

We use a *meter stick* to measure depth. I point out that the centimeter side has more numbers than the inch side. I model all the possible "mistakes" until we agree on how to get accurate measurements: put the end with the low numbers into the water; hold the meter stick straight up and down or vertically. One student will search for and measure the deepest pool of water.

We use a *measuring tape* to measure width. Again I point out the two different measurement scales and model how to retract the metal tape so no one gets hurt. Two students will use the measuring tape to measure the width, from one edge of the water (not the stream bank) to the other. They will try several places to find the widest possible measurement.

We use a *thermometer* to measure the air, water, and snow temperatures. Each measurement is read after counting slowly to one hundred. We review counting by twos when we notice the lines on the thermometer represent two degrees and agree that if the reading is between two lines it is an odd number.

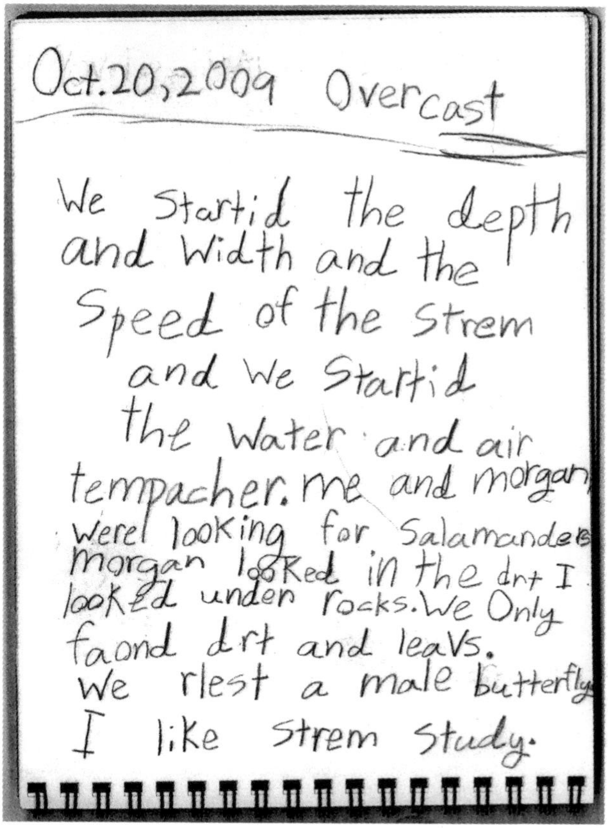

FIGURE 3.17 - Fluent writers are comfortable writing longer journal entries.

> Oct.20, 2009   Overcast
>
> We startid the depth and width and the speed of the strem and we startid the water and air tempacher. me and morgan werel looking for salamandes morgan looked in the dirt I looked under rocks. We Only faond dirt and leavs. We rlest a male butterfly I like strem study.

We use a meter stick, a *timer*, and a *cork* or *Ping-Pong ball* to measure the stream's speed; that is, how many seconds the water flows per meter. We first try a few different places on the streambed until we find a spot where there is enough water flow for the ball to travel along the meter stick without getting hung up. The student holding the timer, a stopwatch, practices starting and stopping it, resetting to zero, and reading the time in minutes, seconds, and tenths of a second. Then one student holds the meter stick steady and releases the cork/ball when the timer says, "Ready, set, go." We calculate the speed at least three times and then take the average measurement. Typically we can measure speed only three or four times a year.

We use *chemical indicators* to measure the health of our stream. This might be done with the whole class in the fall and spring, since buying enough equipment for each group could be costly. Try borrowing a water test kit from a chemistry teacher in your district or try the local pet store for a relatively inexpensive kit. (API [Aquarium Products, Inc.] Master Test Kits include tests for pH, ammonia, nitrite, and nitrate and cost about $20.)

The preliminary discussion about measurement might sound a little different each year.

"What might we notice at the stream as the seasons change?" I ask.

The idea that leaves will turn color and fall off comes up first, then the hope that more animals will appear. In the fall, when we begin our stream observations, the streambed is pretty dry, maybe a puddle or two, so if no one mentions the flow of water, I bring it up myself.

"How might the water in the stream change?" I ask. "What kind of scientific data might we collect about the water?"

And if necessary, "What kind of measurements might we take each month?"

Every year the temperatures vary at different stream sites. When I ask why, there is always a range of ideas. Some students reason: The school building gives off heat so the stream sites closer to the school have warmer air than those farther away; or, the far end of the stream is higher up so it's colder there. Others look for mistakes: Maybe someone did not read the thermometer correctly; or, someone counted to two hundred instead of one hundred. And if no one else thinks of it, I add that our thermometers are not precision tools.

One year we decide to have a student, using the same thermometer, check the temperature at the three stream sites. Not surprisingly, for the adults anyway, the temperatures are identical! When my students, on the other hand, are not particularly interested in the results, I pay attention. I recognize that the power of inquiry is in its ownership. In this case our temperature experiment was driven by my desire to make a teaching point, not my students' curiosity.

This particular year, we never tested the health of our stream. Instead each student learned how to mix chemical indicators; test for ammonia, nitrates, nitrites, and freshwater pH in our trout tank; and record measurements in milligrams per liter.

It occurs to me that I used to allow more time for my students to generate their own ideas about observing change at the stream. Spreading our discussion over several days, I was not as quick to introduce the notion of measurement myself or demonstrate how to use tools for collecting data. Instead I now save time for more follow-up discussion after our stream visits. I consciously value the time spent exploring in the natural world by eliciting my students' observations, discoveries, hypotheses, or simply wonderings. As a teacher, I am constantly making or reevaluating decisions about time management.

CHAPTER 4

A Year at the Stream—Winter

O n warm, sunny fall days you might imagine taking a break now and again from classroom routines to take your students outdoors to explore. But why, you might ask yourself, would I want to continue during the cold, gray months of winter? In fact, our winter stream visits are among my most memorable in all the years of doing nature study. Most of the winter temperatures have actually been quite manageable, and on the occasional frigid day, we simply cut our visit short. And there is something magical about encountering snow in the natural world. My students come alive in the quiet winter wonderland, making snow angels along the banks of a stream transformed into a frozen sheet of ice, examining animal tracks, and digging through the snow to unearth surprising discoveries (see Figure 4.1).

November 21, Ithaca, NY

I eat breakfast watching a blue jay on my bird feeder. For the first time I notice that blue jays cache their seeds. As the blue jay's head goes down, the beak opens up but there's no pecking at the seed to crack it open. The blue jay's head goes up and down, taking a seed each time its beak hits the feeder platform. I count ten to twelve seeds hoarded before the blue jay flies off, only to return for a repeat performance. How did I not notice this before?

TUESDAY, NOVEMBER 10: MINUTE OF SILENCE

We start our day reviewing the October Stream Observations. My students anticipate this well-established routine, so their predictions for today tumble out quickly—squirrels, chipmunks, a family of deer (Samantha thought they might come for a drink of water at the stream), colder water, warmer water, more water, only a big puddle in each stream section, and colder air. I write all predictions on the whiteboard and do not worry that some are contradictory. We will sort it all out when we return from the stream in the afternoon.

FIGURE 4.1 - Children's natural impulse to dig in the snow often leads to unexpected discoveries.

FIGURE 4.2 - Sydney records the most noteworthy observation of the day—"there are so many [leaves] they cover up the stream."

After recess, I introduce the ingenious method for timing speed developed with the help of a parent volunteer and perfected over several years, using a timer, a Ping-Pong ball, and a meter stick.

My students soon fox-walk to their tables, prepare their journal pages, choose measurement jobs, and line up at the door. I put out a collection of extra boots and all four pairs are quickly chosen. Half the class is already out in the hall when I realize I have not reviewed the focus for the day. I call everyone back into the classroom and spontaneously introduce a new strategy—*a minute of silence.*

I want to slow my students down a bit, extend the feeling of quiet reverence for the natural world that we have in the classroom. I have found that my students perform academy-award-winning fox-walks in the woods, but the minute they arrive at their sit spots, the hooting and hollering begins. So I establish a minute of silence at the stream.

"Whoever has the job of measuring speed today will set the timer for one minute as soon as you get to the stream. Everyone will stand in total silence— look up, down, all around, listen, take a deep breath."

I set a timer as I talk, and every fifteen seconds I quietly report how much time has gone by. In this way my students can experience what a minute feels like.

"When the minute is up, please share your observations with everyone in your group. Then do your measurements and then you can explore."

It is a perfect day. November has been unseasonably warm.

"There are leaves everywhere," is the first observation in my group. In fact, leaves cover the entire stream so at first we think there is no water until we realize it is running underneath. Helena adds, "It seems very quiet," and we talk about how different it feels with no leaves on the trees. (See Figure 4.2.)

We begin our second round of measurements. Mia finds the deepest puddle, at six centimeters. Karen, our intrepid parent volunteer who joins us for every stream visit, suggests to Jocelyn and Kaitlyn that Mia's puddle would be a good place to measure the width. Nicholas and Daniel are ready to measure the speed, but it is still not clear whether there is enough running water. Karen and I confer and decide we can measure how long it takes the Ping-Pong ball to travel fifty centimeters, then double it. Repeated trials yield 39, 19, 17, 14, and 7 seconds. Karen explains that when scientists do experiments they usually eliminate the unusual results or *outliers*, in this case, the high of 39 and the low of 7. We decide to double the 14 resulting in a speed of 28 seconds per meter (see Figure 4.3).

These more complicated calculations of averaging and doubling are clearly beyond my second graders' skills. The concept we do work on throughout the year is the relationship between the number of seconds and the speed of the water. Understanding that a lower number of seconds means a faster speed is enough of a challenge, since many children equate a higher number with going faster.

My students take off in all directions once our measurements are recorded. Jocelyn is fascinated with the measuring tape and uses it to measure the length of two logs. Kaitlyn notes that there are so many leaves, she cannot count them all. Victoria sits down to draw some Virginia creeper without leaves to compare

FIGURE 4.3 - A parent helps set up the tools for measuring speed—a cork and a meter stick.

with her previous leafy drawing. I encourage everyone else to look in moist places for signs of life. I start lifting up layers of leaves that have fallen in the stream and a few students join me. We push aside patches of leaves on the stream bank and together we find and identify a spider, a millipede, an empty snail shell, a stonefly or caddisfly (we are not sure which one), and a sow bug. It never feels like we have enough time outside, and soon we are gathering in the circle to share our data.

My group reports 11°C for air temperature. When the other two groups report temperatures in the fifties, I realize they have measured in the Fahrenheit scale. When we stop everything to allow them to change the data, our journaling time is cut short. But as I walk around the room, my students are focused and the entries look adequate. I make a mental note to remind everyone in December that we measure temperature in the Celsius scale, and I wonder how I can better prepare parent volunteers next year.

Reflections

I realize that I need to do a more thorough training for my parent volunteers so after school I take time to reflect on possible topics and prepare a draft:

----

1. Absences—Let me know as soon as possible if you cannot join us. Try to find a substitute if you can. Use the attached substitute list.

2. Plan for the Day—Before we go outside I will review student responsibilities at the stream. Please ask if you are unclear about the instructions and please remind me to give the plan if I forget!

3. Discipline—Students should follow, more or less, the plan I outline right before walking out the door. Let me know right away if a student's behavior is defiant or unsafe.

4. Group Dynamics—Let me know if the dynamics between two or more students make it difficult for the group to work together as a team. From time to time, I will need to make adjustments to the groups I create.

5. Critical Thinking Skills—Instead of giving students immediate answers to their wonderings, ask for their hypotheses first. As much as possible, allow students to discover the natural world on their own. We forget that along with our eager explanations, we teach our students to rely on us, instead of encouraging them to puzzle out problems independently.

I find that from year to year some of the same questions emerge. For example, in November, when late autumn rains finally fill our stream with enough water to flow across the rocks, students wonder where the bubbles come from. One year as we were sharing observations, many students were convinced that the bubbles were "pollution," until Dashiell claimed with authority, "as the stream flows faster, the water swirls around and makes bubbles filled up with air like in waterfalls." I smiled and announced, "You just earned yourself a moment of science, Dashiell." I was so impressed that I decided to ask how he knew about that. He turned toward Deborah, a parent volunteer, saying, "she told us." Clearly this is a delicate balance. We want to benefit from our collective knowledge and experience—teachers, parents, and students alike. I only want to encourage the adults to ask probing questions and allow for some thinking time before giving the answers.

----

6. Nature Journals—Please make your own entries in a nature journal each week. You will not only provide a model for your students but also leave me a snapshot of what happened in your group.

7. Class Historian—Each week we have a new class historian, who is responsible for taking pictures of our life in the classroom and at the stream. We use an old indestructible SONY Mavica camera with floppy disks. Students love taking pictures of the waterfalls, critters, fossils, etc. When the class historian is in your group, please remind her to take about five photos.

Thursday, December 4, Ithaca, NY

Driving home I look up into the sky and see a massive flock of birds at a great distance. Starlings, I think. Are there any other small birds that flock in such great number? And for the hundredth time I also think about how until about five years ago, I would not have noticed. And, again, I feel blessed that I am more aware of the natural world around me.

TUESDAY, DECEMBER 1: LOOKING FOR SIGNS

It is supposed to be a rainy, snowy day so I have not planned for stream study. By 11:30 the weather changes, the sun comes out, and stream study is on! I decide to start by reading aloud Lindsay Barrett George's *In the Woods: Who's Been Here?* and talking about the signs that we might see—clues to the stories that are happening all the time in the natural world.

As always we look at our previous November observations and then make predictions: colder air, leaves on the ground, chipmunks, colder water, way more water.

Daniel adds convincing evidence when he says, "I agree with 'way more water' because there was a big rainstorm a couple of nights ago."

Shaundra says the trees will be naked. I write, "No leaves on the trees."

We read through four clues before I close Barrett's book to groans and protests. The enthusiasm is contagious, but if I keep reading, we will not have enough time outside. (See Chapter 6 for more about literacy and making inferences.)

I review the minute of silence strategy from our prior visit and ask, "What will you do when the timer is set for one minute?"

Chase raises his hand and hesitates, "It's on the tip of my tongue."

"Look around," says Helena.

"Perfect. Remember to look up, down, and across the stream. Notice your observations; look for signs and write down at least three.

My group walks out first today and is impressively quiet. The next two groups come shortly afterward, yakking it up.

"You know, I was just listening to the wind and then, all of a sudden, all I could hear were human voices. Your job is to be absolutely quiet and fox-walk when you enter the woods."

Within minutes of returning to my group, I am thrilled to find some fur-filled scat at my feet. When I choose a focus like "looking for signs," I have learned to trust that something *will* be found—a gift from the natural world. Ninety-five percent of the time, something new and of interest will emerge if you are looking for it. Thinking aloud, Karen wonders if the scat was left by a meat eater (we think raccoon, fox, or skunk), but later, back in the classroom, she wonders if the fur in the scat came instead from a *vegetarian* animal grooming itself.

Karen also finds a heap of white bird droppings. After explaining that birds pee and poop out of the same opening, she helps us infer that this quantity of droppings was not left by a bird passing through, but perhaps by a bird sitting in the tree above, and maybe a large one.

Leaves on the ground riddled with holes fascinate Nicholas. He believes a spider made them, and we talk about other possible leaf-eating insects. I sit with him for ten minutes while we draw and write together. He works steadily and happily incorporates all of my suggestions. I help him add labels—scat, hair, and the slug eating the scat—and encourage him to draw tiny circles in the leaves, which we label "made by insects." What a luxury to have extended time with a student who cannot always engage with such focus and enthusiasm in the classroom.

Leaving Karen in charge for a while, I go to check on my other students. Everyone is happily exploring, but not a single sign has been recorded. I gather the two groups together and ask whether their temperature data matches our predictions.

When they seem to be guessing, I ask, "How can you be sure?"

"Aha," says Noah, "We can look in our books."

Everyone checks their data charts where the numbers prove that the air and water temperatures are in fact colder in December than in November.

"Okay, let's start looking for signs," I announce, taking in the woods and stream with an inviting sweep of my arms. It does not take long to find signs, and inferences tumble out of my students' mouths: Holes in a log? Must be a woodpecker. Pieces of nutshell on a log? Squirrel. A hole at the base of a tree? Squirrel home. A log with bark scraped away? Made by a deer with its antlers. Maple sap? Maple syrup season must be coming soon (see Figure 4.4). When everyone is writing and drawing in their journals, the parents quietly thank me, and as I walk away, I realize that although I am not ready to restructure the stream groups, I do need to keep better tabs on how the parent-led groups are functioning.

When we return to the classroom we still have time to record the rest of our observations and share three signs from each group. And everyone remembers to report temperature in the Celsius scale: 8°C for air; 6°C for water.

Reflections

After school I allow a few moments to cherish the day. My timing, for once, is impeccable. I always try to have our first stream discussion in the morning when we list our predictions. In the afternoon, I introduce the focus of the day, present a teaching point or two, read part of a book, or tell a personal story. I am ever mindful of the clock so that our preliminary discussions do not run too long. Twenty to thirty minutes is the maximum sit-time for my students. Today it all worked: I pulled off a last-minute plan; we did not feel rushed outside; and in the classroom, there was still time to journal and share many noteworthy signs.

But on my way home from school I rerun the movie of the two mischievous stream groups and wonder what went wrong. These are good kids who love the natural world and usually follow the "plan," eager to share their exciting discoveries. One parent is a stream study veteran and the other has established a good rapport with her crew. Are my expectations unrealistic?

FIGURE 4.4 - My students learn that although we may not always find answers, there is value to our questions in the natural world. Here Sydney records signs—*scat, cut, lots of leaves, seed, hole,* and *mysteries (mistre).*

As I pull into my driveway, my questions return to critical-thinking skills and parent involvement. My stream group benefits enormously from Karen's expertise about animals, and I welcome her instinctive teaching moments. Today she waited to make her observations about meat eaters (the animal's prey being the source of the fur) until after my students had offered their own ideas. When she later changed her mind (the fur coming from a vegetarian mammal grooming itself), I was able to point out that scientists generate multiple hypotheses when problem solving. Isn't the process of wondering together what I am striving for?

I remind myself that teaching is an art, an ever-evolving one, and revisit my thoughts about routines and parent involvement and even critical-thinking skills. Of course, routines can be flexible. Of course, parents are among the experts who teach us and model their own thinking. Of course, my students do not have to figure out everything by themselves. And finally, children, including seven- and eight-year-olds, will be children sometimes! My job is to reflect on my teaching practice, observe and listen carefully to my students, continue a dialogue with parents, and be open to change.

What I love about teaching is the ability to meander down new learning paths with my students. My passion for the natural world and my desire to instill that passion in my students are what drive our nature study curriculum. I believe that visiting our sit spots in small groups nurtures a more intimate connection with nature. Perhaps my students are more focused and productive when under my watchful eye, yet I have to trust that they will continue to discover, learn, and savor the natural world without me.

Sunday, January 11, Providence, RI

There is a bird feeder set up very close to the window where we eat break-fast each morning. Mostly house sparrows show up—a dozen or more. I am surprised to find that up close, this ubiquitous city bird is quite attractive, each one perched on the peak of a picket fence slat. One or two at a time, chickadee, downy woodpecker, junco, nuthatch, blue jay, and cardinal all stop for a brief visit. When a single robin suddenly appears on a tree branch in the neighbor's yard, I can almost smell the fresh breath of spring air. The robin flies to the picket fence, and against a backdrop of bright orange siding, the robin dazzles, most elegant of birds. More support for the "less is more" theory. On an ordinary day in April, three robins in the garden do not evoke such a response.

TUESDAY, JANUARY 12: TRACKS IN THE SNOW

When I look out the window this morning, the abundance of squirrel tracks in the freshly fallen snow catches my attention. What a perfect follow-up to our December focus on signs. Today we will search for tracks in the snow and imagine what stories *they* tell.

After recess I meet my students in the hall and announce, "Hang up your coats but don't take off your snow pants or boots. We're going outside for stream study today."

We gather in the circle, where I remind them about our December stream study, Lindsay Barrett George's book *In the Woods: Who's Been Here?*, and how we looked for signs. I ask each group to share one.

"I found fur and inferred that a raccoon rubbed against a log trying to get away from a predator," remembers Sydney.

"We found a large amount of bird droppings and my mom inferred that a flock of birds, maybe crows, had been perching up above," contributes Daniel.

Eric recalls, "We found a hole at the bottom of a tree and think an animal used to live there."

Over and over again I am gratified by the power of these experiences for my students, who remember them in detail.

Our book today is *How to Be a Nature Detective* by Millicent E. Selsam. My students love the challenge of identifying tracks—snake, frog, and rabbit. We learn that rabbits jump with their front legs placed in between their hind legs so their tracks present the hind legs first. My students use this information successfully to figure out which way the rabbit is going in the illustration. Once again I am torn between finishing the book and getting us outside with enough time to enjoy our first snowy exploration.

"Is there any way we could measure the snow today?" I wonder aloud.

"How fast it's falling?" asks Sabina.

"If you figure out a way to do that, let me know," I quickly respond, moving on to the next suggestion.

When the more mundane ideas of depth and temperature are suggested, we review our tools and agree to add those to our measurements today.

I decide to leave the journals inside. Remembering the disaster of September rain, I imagine they will not fare well sitting on a snowy log. With a reminder to hold a minute of silence at their stream sites, we head outside. We stay together and joyfully plow through the two-foot-deep snow behind the school. There are tracks everywhere.

When Daniel excitedly yells, "deer track, deer track," we stop and speculate why a deer might have stopped right next to a tree.

"It was peeing there?"

"Maybe rubbing its antler there?"

Cynthia, the Red group's parent leader, thinks it is too big for a deer track. We take a few minutes to ponder why accurate identification might be tricky.

FIGURE 4.5 - My stream group observes a minute of silence at our sit spot.

Snow melting and refreezing can alter the size of tracks over time. Or tracks can look bigger because a heavy animal like a deer sinks deeply into the snow. From here we enter the woods, lifting our legs high with each step, turning off the path toward our respective stream sites.

While observing the minute of silence, my group notices more tracks on the opposite stream bank (see Figure 4.5). Daniel is beside himself, "It's amazing, Laurie. We just read that book and we're seeing tracks, and last time we read about signs and we saw scat!"

"We sure are lucky, Daniel!" I agree.

We manage to do our measurements, but soon the lure of the fresh white snow is intoxicating (see Figures 4.6 and 4.7). Daniel and Nicholas dig in the snow, making slush in the streambed and a big enough hole to measure the depth of the water. Kids are flopping down and making snow angels. Chunks of snow are flying. Jocelyn falls, laughing too hard to get back up. Later she puts snow in the low crotch of a tree, yelling, "Look Laurie, an egg."

We all play hard and though the thought *great writing possibilities* slips through my brain, for once I make the command decision that we will stay out as long as possible and worry about journaling tomorrow.

FIGURE 4.6 - FIGURE 4.7 - During the winter months we measure the temperature and depth of the snow.

Reflections

After school I read these notes in Lisa's parent journal:

We saw an established deer path, which showed us that deer had gone back and forth from someone's garden through the woods.

Sabina found rabbit tracks leading into the hollow log where last month we found some raccoon or fox tracks.

Noah discovered a pinecone so large it didn't seem to be from around here. Luis and Olivia guessed it might have come from California.

Lisa's Blue group was, excuse the pun, right on track! They followed the plan discussing hypotheses about various tracks and the giant pinecone. All my worrying last month about the focus of parent-led groups now seems unfounded.

I return to Sabina's suggestion about measuring how fast the snow is falling and feel my stomach lurch as I remember my flip response. Of course we cannot be perfect mentors all the time, but as much as possible I try to validate my students' creative thinking. A better comeback might have been, "Let's come back to that another day and figure out a good measurement strategy together."

Before leaving for the day, I write instructions on the whiteboard followed by a list of measurements, including snow depth and temperature: "Take out your nature journals. Record your observations at the stream yesterday. Please write your measurement data on the board."

The next morning about half a dozen young naturalists take out their journals and carefully record their data. When everyone else arrives, I set aside another fifteen minutes for updating our journals (see Figure 4.8).

A similar scenario happened the year before when we relished the snow as long as possible and recorded in our journals the following day. That year we had four stream groups and one managed to cut through the ice, find enough water to measure, and record a speed of fifteen seconds per meter.

"Is that slow or fast?" I asked.

"Fast," everyone agreed.

We took a quick look at nature journals from the three other stream groups and found December speeds of four, seven, and five seconds.

"Now that you have more data, what do you think about fifteen seconds?" I continued.

A few students confidently changed their opinions to "slow or slower" but the rest of the class was not so sure. Again we talked about how confusing it is that the larger number in this case means it takes longer for the cork (or Ping-Pong ball) to move down the stream, translating to a slower speed.

We also reviewed the temperatures. Many remembered that zero degrees Celsius means thirty-two degrees Fahrenheit, but I realized that the significance of these reference points was lost on them.

"Zero degrees means freezing," offered Ariella.

"Freezing what?"

"I don't know."

FIGURE 4.8 - Sydney draws several kinds of tracks and a deer path—"it had been walked on so many times that it made a path."

We reviewed what was different about the stream this time—it was frozen. I explained that water freezes at 0°C and 32°F and made a mental note to come back to this idea at regular intervals throughout the year.

Although it might take time for my students to internalize these measurement concepts, I believe that collecting stream measurement data as scientists is a more tangible experience and an essential complement to more arbitrary measurements performed in the classroom or on the workbook page.

January is the sweet spot of the academic year. Most students come back from December vacation relaxed, more peaceful, happy to see their friends, and ready to learn. Routines are well established; a comfortable rhythm permeates the day. Similarly our January stream study feels effortless and uncomplicated. We get the job done, but everyone, adults included, has fun!

Thursday, February 12, Ithaca, NY

I pull into my driveway at 6:00 p.m. and the crows are back! I estimate 1,000 or more. I count 100 inside the crotch of two branches. There are at least three more crotches in that tree and then another whole tree besides. Having recently seen Hitchcock's The Birds, *I am plunged right back inside that story. But I am not afraid of these birds as much as fascinated about why they are appearing in such great numbers this year and what they are doing when they flock up like that. I continue emptying the many grocery bags from the trunk of my car. As I carry the last load, a sound like a gun blast startles me, and I look up to see all 1,000 plus crows take off to a neighborhood due north. What spooked them? And why did only four crows decide to stay put? I continue to learn to ask questions of the natural world, to put together a story. I try to practice what I am asking my students to do.*

TUESDAY, FEBRUARY 2: ICE AT THE STREAM

I spend my lunch hour thinking, again, about how to maximize the nature journaling experience so that my students will take their time writing more focused entries. A month ago I wrote in my planning book, "Out the door by 12:35 p.m., back inside by 1:15 p.m.," already anticipating a more relaxed journaling time. I decide to take our journals outside today.

After recess, we review our January stream observations, and I remind my students that these notes reflect big changes from December to January. Our prediction list today reads: one big sheet of ice, patches of ice, some water flowing slowly, maybe a salamander, leaves on the ground, wet ground.

The plan on the board reads:

1. One minute of silence to listen and observe
2. Measurements
3. Explorations
4. Nature journals—write or draw about three small moments you experience

We make it outside by 12:45 p.m. The ice is thrilling—a giant sheet from one end of the stream to the other. Nicholas calls it shiny. I only assign air temperature to Daniel and width of the ice to Victoria and Kaitlyn because it seems doubtful we will be measuring any water today.

Pretty soon kids are skating, slipping, sliding, and falling on their bottoms all over the place. I brace myself, trying not to worry about injuries and let it happen, hoping their puffy snow gear will provide some protection. In the adjoining Red group, three or four students are sliding down a solid waterfall of ice and struggle to climb back up the slippery incline.

"Climb up along the bank," I yell across the icy expanse.

Kaitlyn and Daniel manage to crash through the ice and take a measurement for the depth of the deepest pool at nine centimeters (see Figure 4.9). The width of the ice is 220 centimeters. I put out new thermometers, but they are just as unreliable as the old ones—the air temperature of 2°C seems suspect since our school weather station registered 27°F.

FIGURE 4.9 - Students are excited to break through the ice and measure the water depth.

FIGURE 4.10 - Students sit on a log at their sit spot to record observations.

Soon all my students are exploring. Many are reciting Douglas Florian's poem (from his book *Winter Eyes*), "Icicles are dragon's teeth. They don't grow up. They drip beneath" (1999, 25). After about ten minutes I work my way up and down the ice gathering everyone together, declaring the ice off limits and breathing a sigh of relief that no one was hurt.

It is warm enough to write in our journals outside without freezing our fingers (see Figure 4.10). Everyone is pretty focused. They write about the tracks in the snow, holes in the ice—a winter home for a salamander, Leslie speculates—and the discovery that ice freezes in layers. Jocelyn finds a beautiful fossil—part of a brachiopod, I believe. I give her a quick lesson about how fossils were formed millions of years ago.

We leave the stream at 1:20 p.m., only ten minutes behind my intended schedule. Not too bad. Inside, everyone gathers in the circle, where I share three student journal entries from the week before—detailed, labeled drawings and short, concise narratives. As we end the day, everyone finishes their journal entries with these models in mind (see Figure 4.11).

Reflections

"Put your fossil in a safe place, Jocelyn," I remind her as we approach the line of yellow school buses and shake hands good-bye. I find myself smiling and enjoying the crisp air as I turn and walk slowly up the sidewalk, newly cleared of ice. Our visit to the stream today has filled me up like a visit to an old friend, the kind where the conversation resumes effortlessly after months or even years apart. My students were giddy as they investigated every possible property of ice! In fact, we did not need a particular focus today beyond the ice that nature provided. Our observations, measurements, explorations, play, and journaling

FIGURE 4.11 - Today most journal entries focus on the ice—thick and thin and a great place to slide!

all felt leisurely. We did skip our culminating discussion, but it is simply not possible to do everything.

All the way back to the classroom my students were talking quietly among themselves. Here and there, stomping through the snow, they nodded to each other, "Stream study is fun."

Thursday, March 15, Wood Street, Ithaca, NY

The grackles are back and the geese are flying north. Thought I heard grackles in Ray's Norway spruce yesterday. Today the first grackle is on my feeder, magnificent, metallic blue feathers flashing, with a seemingly proud demeanor. Soon I'll be knocking on the windowpane to chase them away in hopes of making room for other songbirds, but today they are the harbingers of spring.

TUESDAY, MARCH 2: SURPRISES

By March we are usually looking for signs of spring, but today the ground is snow-covered, a perfect opportunity to revisit our investigation of tracks and inferences. Before leaving for music class we take a few moments to practice, and everyone finds a spot along the wall of windows looking out on the woods. Shaundra points out tracks going from the bird feeder to the woods and infers *squirrels*.

"What is the evidence for your inference?" I ask.

"We see squirrels all the time!" she answers with authority.

In fact, Shaundra sits right next to the window where she has been observing and writing about squirrels all year. Samantha then infers it could be only *one* squirrel going back and forth, creating a path that looks like a tunnel in the snow.

"Where might the squirrel be coming from? Where do squirrels go in winter?" I continue.

"They hibernate," says Leslie.

"What does it mean to hibernate?" I ask, hoping Leslie will figure out by herself why this would make our squirrel sightings impossible.

When Luis explains that animals sleep all winter and kind of wake up in the spring, Leslie quickly realizes her mistake, and I make a note to find a book about squirrels for my next read-aloud.

After recess we record the date and weather on a new journal page and choose measuring jobs. Remembering the lineup of wet journals on the windowsill last month, I decide the student journals will stay inside, leaving the adults to record the measurements.

"If you don't have running water, remember to measure the depth and temperature of the snow. And remember the inferences you made this morning about the squirrel tracks? Look for tracks today and imagine what stories they tell."

Without further discussion we head outside, and I see that the snow has melted away from the brick wall of the school, leaving a ready-made path.

"Please walk close to the school," I point out. "That way we won't disturb any tracks we might find in the snow."

We stop often on the way to the stream to examine tracks crisscrossing the deep snow. The nail prints are visible in the squirrel tracks. I catch up to a group looking at tracks where the larger footprints are in front and the smaller ones in back. With a parent's help, the Blue group is remembering what they learned about rabbits and squirrels, whose smaller front legs are placed behind their larger back legs as they jump. With this information they immediately figure out in which direction the squirrel was going.

When my group enters the woods, over a foot of heavy, icy snow makes for slow, ponderous walking. We observe a minute of silence when we arrive at our sit spot, and then the measurements go pretty quickly because our site is totally frozen over. I set off to visit the other two groups and find Samantha and Paige standing next to a patch of dried leaves uncovered from the melting snow. Samantha infers that a deer must have rested there because she has already observed this phenomenon at her house. Since there are three large patches of exposed leaves, Samantha thinks at least three deer were sleeping here, or maybe four, if a baby was sleeping with its mother (see Figure 4.12). I do not bother pointing out that this is not the season for baby deer. Instead I call the rest of their group over to enjoy this discovery and soon everyone is noticing the deer tracks around the resting places.

Kaitlyn, a shy girl who rarely raises her hand in class to venture an opinion or an original idea, appears at my side and quietly tells me that she found some blood in the snow. I quickly return to my group and sure enough, on the opposite side of the bank, the snow has some spots of pinkish red. Daniel and his

FIGURE 4.12 - Students continue to make inferences to answer the question, "What happened here?"

mom are already digging, and in less than a minute they find hair, some meaty bones, and then an unmistakable rabbit nose with a few whiskers attached. The nose is a bit disturbing, so we bury it again but take some of the bones to share with the rest of the class. On our way back, as we wait for a parent to open the back door for us, we hit the jackpot—a red-tailed hawk flies through the woods and perches on a visible tree.

Since it is close to dismissal, my students keep their boots and snow pants on. We make a circle of chairs, and with pencil and journal in hand, everyone finds a seat (see Figure 4.13). We share some of our stories and Kaitlyn walks the bones around the circle. Realizing that the oral storytelling will serve as a prompt for many of my reluctant writers, I announce, "It is time to open your journals and write down one of these stories. No talking please, for ten minutes."

About two-thirds of the class is focused and independent. Most write about the red-tailed hawk or the bunny. Others need a jump-start, redirection, or just encouragement to keep writing. I crouch down in front of Jocelyn, who has drawn a tree with leaves on it.

"Did you see a tree like that today, Jocelyn? Remember, we are recording what we *actually* saw today."

She chooses to write about the bunny nose, and I move on to help Nicholas organize his thoughts. After ten minutes, several entries are shared, and we have just enough time to record measurements before walking to the buses.

Later, as I transfer the whiteboard predictions to our paper chart of year-long stream observations, I realize that I can award two moments of science tomorrow—to Samantha for discovering the deer resting places and to Kaitlyn for the small patch of blood leading to bones and hair. I again appreciate the surprises the natural world always has in store for us. I am confident that this day filled with exciting new discoveries will translate into stories my students will tell for many years to come (see Figure 4.14).

FIGURE 4.13 - Eager to record the surprises of the day, my students write with focus and stamina.

FIGURE 4.14 - Kaitlyn records all of the day's surprises—the red-tailed hawk, the deer resting places, and the bunny remains.

Reflections

Usually stream study happens in mid-March when we look for signs of spring. So this year, not wanting to wait until April when spring would be much further along, I plan a walk outside the following week when most of the snow has already melted.

We review the list of possible signs of spring that we brainstormed in the morning—birds singing, snowdrop flowers growing, snow melting, more sunny days—before putting on our coats and heading out behind the school. It is a clear sunny day, and it feels like we won the lottery to be going outside again so soon.

The first stop is our bird feeder, where we find grass growing up between the sunflower seed shells, and excited shouts of "sign of spring" reverberate around the circle of happy children. We note dandelions and birds singing.

The moss is growing new leaves and looks greener. I am pleased that, when we approach the remaining patches of snow, my students instinctively start identifying tracks and hypothesizing. Daniel finds clumps of hair and theorizes that animals are shedding. I am even more delighted when Sydney counters (even though Daniel is viewed as something of a nature expert) with the possibility that an animal was being chased; some of its fur was bitten off and then left on the ground.

We walk around to the front of the school where we find signs of spring in the flower beds—daffodil leaves and other sprouting bulbs. "A purple flower, a purple flower," yells Jocelyn to get my attention. It turns out to be a dead bud from the previous year, and I realize that my students do not understand how plants grow. Unfortunately we no longer teach plant life cycles as part of the second-grade science curriculum, so I make a note to be on the lookout for buds, flowers, and fruits on our remaining stream study days.

CHAPTER 5

A Year at the Stream—Spring

Nature study in the springtime is enticing for a variety of reasons. First, with the return to warmer weather, we are less encumbered by our gear and take pleasure in a lighter step and freer movement. The warmer temperatures also bring back the wild plants and animals—insects in various stages of their life cycles, salamanders, and the green sprouts of perennial plants poking through dried leaves on the forest floor. Students who were a bit uneasy with our first autumn stream visits can be found happily digging in the spring mud or at least tripping lightly to their sit spots, eager for change. Finally, in the natural world as in the classroom, my students now follow well-established routines, understand teacher expectations, and (most of the time) practice acceptable behaviors. Trusting that my students will find their own way, their own focus, and their own joy, I offer minimal instruction before we step outside together, five senses open, flexing our naturalist muscles.

TUESDAY, APRIL 13: CHOOSING NAMES FROM THE NATURAL WORLD

When I first began nature study at the stream, I marked off the group sit spots by tying different colors of yarn around tree trunks. I simply used colors as group names so that I could keep track of who was where. Along the way, I thought it would be better to have the children choose their own site names, something from the natural world. It is not until April this year, when parent volunteers are in the classroom and we are not going outside, that I remember to introduce the idea to my students.

"We have spent a lot of time together in the natural world. We have studied about birds; now we are studying insects; we have met so many plants and animals at the stream. Today I would like you to choose a name for your stream group—the only rule is that the name has to come from the natural world. What categories can we list?" I ask to begin the brainstorming that will soon transfer to each group.

"Birds."

"Insects."

"Yes, your name could be some kind of animal."

"Trees."

"Yes, a type of plant."

"We named our rural community Green Meadow."

"Yes, it could be part of a natural landscape—a meadow or forest or beach."

There is much excited chatter and the names are chosen quickly. The Green group chooses Green Trees. The Blue group, unable to come to consensus, puts all of their ideas together—Blue Maple Chipmunks.

Lisa calls me over for assistance and asks, "Does it have to be a real animal?"

When I answer, yes, they cross out "Blue," then "Maple," and stay with "Chipmunks." I work with the Red group today, which starts with the category of birds. Possibilities are Pileated Woodpecker, Northern Cardinal, Blue Jay, Red-headed Woodpecker, Bald Eagle, and Tufted Titmouse. I give each student two votes. On the first round Bald Eagle has the most votes and Tufted Titmouse is eliminated. By the second round all votes are for Bald Eagle except Shaundra, who graciously gives up her choice of Blue Jay.

From now on we are known as the Green Trees, the Chipmunks, and the Bald Eagles.

Sunday, April 19, Stewart Park, Ithaca, NY

I spot something black and white in the canal that runs under the bridges. I expect a common merganser since I've seen them here before so what a treat to find a hooded merganser looking back at me through my binoculars. No mistaking its white, black-bordered hood. I watch it lifting its crest in a mating posture and wonder where the mate is. I am just about to leave when the mate shows up and starts bobbing her head vigorously, lifting herself right out of the water vertically with a flapping of her wings. And then, just as I am about to leave again, an unmistakable wood duck shows up and swims majestically toward the mergansers. "Be patient and stay a while" is one of the tips I regularly share with my students.

TUESDAY, APRIL 20: NATURALISTS ON THEIR OWN

Yesterday after school, I strode into the woods to look around for a stream study focus. I was happy for the excuse to get outside for even ten minutes—my favorite kind of planning! I slowed down at the stream's bank taking in the sights, sounds, and smells. In the middle of the stream I found a small log, actually a piece of firewood escaped from our neighbor's woodpile, covered with giant cream-colored fungi. I admired the splashes of color—mayapples and other wildflowers in bloom—and when the robins started singing, it was an irresistible invitation to revisit the signs of spring.

In the morning, we examine the section titled "Eastern Spring" in *Woods Walk* by Henry W. Art and Michael W. Robins. Brightly colored photos show ferns, mushrooms, flowers, sow bugs (also called wood lice), nests, and the changing colors of the trees. We relish the photo of the porcupine—our favorite character, Ereth, in the Poppy series—even though we do not expect to see one.

Then Mia reminds me to tell everyone about the red-bellied woodpecker nest. A week ago I had seen a red-bellied at the feeder and watched it fly twice to the same spot on the red oak outside our window, the one we call the "V Tree" because it has two trunks slanting away from each other in the shape of a *V*. On a hunch, I went out after school to see if I could find a nest in the tree. When I bumped into Mia and her mom, they decided to join me. Unfortunately we did not find anything, but today I ask our woodpecker experts (Daniel, Chase, and

Eric chose woodpeckers as their nonfiction book topics) where woodpeckers might make their nests. Daniel reports that they excavate nests in tree cavities so we plan to have another look on the way to the stream.

We fox-walk right to the V tree hoping to find the red-bellied nest. Four students in each group hold on to the binoculars dangling around their necks to keep them from bouncing off their chests. We tilt our heads to gaze up the length of the red oak, but if there is indeed a nest filled with baby woodpeckers, a dead branch sticking straight up in front of it obscures our view.

We continue to the stream where we do our measurements first, each scientist checking in with me before recording her findings. When Victoria reports an air temperature over 20°C, it seems too high and we realize she put her thermometer in the sun. She tries again in the shade and this time gets 15°C, concurring with Noah's earlier meteorologist report from the school weather station. I like the flow of our visit today as we move on to exploring next. When stream visits start with open explorations, it is often challenging to coax my students away from their discoveries to begin measuring.

Now, Nicholas digs in the ground for about five minutes before he pops up, very excited, with something pink. Victoria recognizes it as a larva similar to the larvae of the pink lady butterflies in our classroom.

"These larvae move in the same way, by stretching themselves out," she explains to Nicholas, who goes on to unearth a cherry pit hull, and one find after another.

"What's this, what's this?" he asks over and over again. His engagement in the natural world is so unlike his behavior in the classroom, where he becomes engrossed with his fingers, picking at dead skin while I introduce a lesson or read a book.

Jocelyn finds two snails that she holds carefully in her hands.

"Laurie, are darkling beetles older than us?" she asks, referring to the beetles that recently hatched in our classroom.

"What do you mean, Jocelyn? They've only been around a few weeks."

She flashes me a big grin.

"But they're adults!"

When Jocelyn makes a joke about the adult stage of the mealworms she has so enjoyed observing during free choice times, I realize she has mastered her understanding of insect life cycles. She then asks about ripples in the water. I point out the difference between running water and still water as we move up the stream. When she looks puzzled, I show her how the rippling water is always moving across the rocks, just as Helena appears at my side with an urgent request.

"Come listen to the water in the waterfall, Laurie. It sounds like it's whistling" (see Figure 5.1).

I listen with my eyes closed and slowly break into a smile. "Thank you so much for calling me over to hear that beautiful sound, Helena."

When everyone in the Green Trees group has had a chance to explore at a leisurely pace, we sit down on our log together to record all the measurements. In addition to Victoria, Kaitlyn reports water temperature at 13°C; Nicholas and Daniel turn in a width of 176 centimeters; Helena's depth is 5.5 centimeters; Mia and Jocelyn submit a speed of nine seconds per meter.

FIGURE 5.1 - The diminutive waterfalls along our stream are a source of delight for everyone.

"Can you find another month where the measurements are close to what we found today?" I ask.

It does not take very long for my students to check their data charts and find similar measurements in November (157 centimeters width, 6 centimeters depth), December (seven seconds per meter speed) and October (14°C air temperature.) We agree that we must have had similar weather in the fall.

Not wanting to go inside just yet on such a beautiful day, I decide spontaneously that we will share our discoveries outside, with each group taking a turn to host the rest of the class. The Chipmunks share wood lice and the soil inside a log, ants, and a patch of delicate yellow blossoms. I cannot resist inviting everyone to draw the flowers, and what ensues is my absolutely favorite scenario in the natural world—students gathered around, nature journals in hand, quietly observing and drawing, with baskets of colored pencils close by (see Figure 5.2). They work hard as artists, making representational drawings and enjoying the opportunity to add color. Some students draw the whole patch; others move closer and draw one blossom in more detail. Before progressing to the next group, we also visit the patch of mayapples, where Chase declares, "They look just like little palm trees" (see Figure 5.3).

The Bald Eagles show us daffodils and vinca, convinced they are wildflowers. I take time to explain that sometimes the intentional human world intersects with the wild natural world. Although people most likely planted these flowers, they spread very easily into natural areas.

The Green Trees decide to share a sapling that Daniel found. To my disappointment I was apparently the only one intrigued by the mushrooms on the piece of firewood.

After cleanup, we gather in the circle to examine the cracked, light-blue eggshell Samantha found on the way in. Although everyone thinks it is an American robin's egg, I persevere in modeling thorough research by opening the Peterson's nest field guide I keep close at hand. To our surprise, we discover that starlings, bluebirds, and house finches also lay blue eggs, although of different lengths.

"Why don't you measure it?" suggests Jade.

I place the egg on a piece of white paper on the carpet with a centimeter ruler alongside and invite Samantha to come up and take a reading. Everyone is smiling when the approximate three-centimeter length confirms our original guess.

FIGURE 5.2 - A patch of lesser celandine, an invasive plant, provides inspiration for representational drawing.

Reflections

There is much to celebrate about nature study at this point in the year. At the top of the list is my students' proficiency as naturalists. The constant reminder to observe and question in the natural world has clearly paid off. They no longer rely on me to show them the way, and if truth be told, they are more likely to bypass my interests altogether (witness the fungi on the log), eager to return to or pursue their own fascinations. From the minute my students step on to the grass and until they walk back inside the school, they are on the lookout! They need no more coaxing or encouraging. As a matter of fact, they are unstoppable. Starting with the search for tracks in a few patches of snow two weeks ago, to Helena's whistling waterfall, to Samantha's egg discovered just moments before entering the school building, there is no discrete beginning or end to nature study for these watchful second graders. When they are in the natural world, they are all eyes . . . and ears, noses, and hands as well.

My most challenged students, Jocelyn and Nicholas, also share this competence. During our weekly, and then monthly, stream visits, not only do they look like everyone else in the class, but also there are times when everyone is looking to them as the experts. They have learned to make observations independently, and, in the context of the natural world, they have been able to internalize important scientific concepts. Whether outside at the stream or back in our classroom, I value these opportunities to support them, strengthen their writing skills, and enjoy their company in an environment that gives all of us deep pleasure.

After seven months at the stream, we have enough measurements to examine our data over time, make comparisons, and begin to think about the changes in water as the seasons unfold. We can move from specific measurement tasks to

FIGURE 5.3 - A student draws and labels a variety of plants— "algae or moss, Mayapple, yellow" (for the Celandine) and "baby tree."

a more complex synthesis of our statistics. Together with the class job of mete-orologist—a student who creates a daily weather report based on observation of the sky as well as the temperature and wind speed from our school weather station—my students receive a more comprehensive overview of weather, which is one of the second-grade science units at my school.

Now that our procedures are so well established at the stream, it is a welcome change for everyone to diverge from our usual routine. It is fun to travel together today. A vibrant energy accompanies each visit to new territory. My students delight in our spontaneous artistic gathering in the woods because after months of my modeling and highlighting representational drawing, they are ready to meet the challenge.

Last year we did something similar when there was very little water to measure. We took only one measurement basket outside and stayed together as a class. As one group did measurements at their own site, the other groups explored. When a student discovered something interesting, everyone stopped and came over to take a look—rotted newspaper that looked like mold, giant worms, a salamander, or a sprouting seed. Yet then and now, I cannot ignore the effort it takes to keep twenty-one active children relatively quiet and together in one spot, which affirms my instinct to separate into small groups for most of the year.

I am eager to share the day's highlights with my partner, David, tonight, and already feel a bit wistful when I realize there are only two stream study days left in the school year.

Wednesday, May 11, Belle Sherman Woods, Ithaca, NY

It has been about six weeks since Gabriel* and I walked together. We feel blessed by this beautiful spring day. The woods welcome us with greenery and yellow, purple, and white flowers; a gently flowing stream; and birdsong everywhere. Gabriel takes off his sneakers, wades in the perfectly cool water, and tries to catch a frog. In the end, he is picking skinny leeches off his feet. It is only then that we discover a whole "colony" of leeches in a smear of mud on a large flat rock. I wander down the stream, picking up flat rocks until I find what I think are caddis fly homes—clusters of tiny pebbles held together by mud. I notice a slight opening in the mud on one end.

Gabriel is the fifth-grade son of dear friends and he is also a struggling writer. In my first year of retirement from teaching, knowing that the teacher/ student relationship is what I will miss most, I offer to tutor him once a week using nature journals to practice writing.

TUESDAY, MAY 18: INSECTS EVERYWHERE

Rain is forecast for today, but I cannot cancel stream study because it is the last possible Tuesday available in May. When my students return early from outdoor recess, I glance at the light rain falling outside and resolve to get ready for stream study on the spot. I pass out the nature journals and circulate throughout the room helping each group choose their measurement jobs for the day.

"This is our last stream study!"

A disappointed echo travels around the room as everyone notices that May is the last month on our weather data chart. I assure everyone that we will absolutely visit the stream one more time in June. Karen, Lisa, and Cynthia arrive just as we are finishing up. Fortunately about half a dozen kids brought full rain gear and almost everyone else has decent footwear. I hand out my entire supply of plastic red, blue, and green rain ponchos, and we head outside, hoping to elude a downpour (see Figure 5.4).

Thanks to the warm 56°F (13°C) temperature, it is quite pleasant to be out in the drizzle. The plan is to do measurements right away and then decide whether we can stay outside long enough to explore. We have left the student journals inside and the adults are prepared to record the new data. My group is about to start measuring when Victoria asks, "Laurie, are we going to do the one-minute thing?" Ah, the wisdom of eight-year-olds and their love of routine. In my rush to beat the rain, I forgot about our minute of silence. We are just recovering from Kaitlyn's running, taking a flying leap through the air, and falling to the ground, so it is just what we need to slow us down. Helena starts the timer; we stop, listen, and take in the birdsong.

There is enough water to measure speed today—twelve seconds per meter, three seconds slower than in April (see Figure 5.5). When Jocelyn and Victoria finish measuring what turns out to be our shortest width of the year at forty-two centimeters, everyone is ready to look for salamanders.

FIGURE 5.4 - Far from a deterrent, the light rain makes us hopeful that salamanders will be plentiful today.

Soon Nicholas finds a fat, juicy larva in the water, and I realize that I should have asked everyone to look for signs of insect life and the life cycles that we are in the midst of studying. Apparently my reminder is not necessary because my students proceed to find evidence of insects everywhere.

Jocelyn is the first to shout, "Larvae, larvae," when I show Nicholas's catch to my group. Again I marvel at how the scientific vocabulary, usually so difficult for special education students, rolls effortlessly off her tongue. Earlier in the day Jocelyn was the one who noticed a single white web forming in the corner of the silkworm habitat in our classroom. When she shared it with the class I let her be the first to hypothesize.

"Jocelyn, what do you think is going on here?"

"Pupae!" was her immediate response. Jocelyn may not understand Latin plurals, but she is absolutely clear about the stages of an insect's life cycle.

Daniel and Kaitlyn spend the whole time trying to catch a salamander and ultimately succeed. Paige finds a leaf with perfectly round yellow bumps on its underside as well as a small cocoon in the middle of a nutshell.

The rain cooperates and we stay outside until we run out of time. On the way back, always looking for chances to inspire critical thinking, I stop the class in front of a tall patch of grass.

"What can you infer here? Why is there tall grass right here and nowhere else?" I prompt.

My students are used to this routine and start thinking.

"More rain was falling here."

"Maybe there is more compost here."

"There are less trees here so more sun is shining through," comes from Jade.

I want to break into song as my students build on each other's hypotheses and are willing to take risks, and as new voices join in, not just the usual ones.

FIGURE 5.5 - A student waits for the "ready, set, go" before releasing a cork to time the speed of the running water.

"What good thinking. You just named everything that a plant needs in order to grow—water, good soil, and sunshine."

Back in the classroom everyone has ten minutes to write down his or her own experience at the stream—what they found, what they saw. Again I am pleased at the overall quality of the entries (see Figure 5.6).

When Victoria opens her journal, she points to the silkworm larva she drew the week before.

"I'm really proud of this one," she says as she points to the accurate detail she included—prolegs, true legs, and the thirteen segments.

I draw lines on the blank page for Nicholas and help him remember what he found at the stream. Then we prepare orally for what he will write—"I found a larva in the water." While we are working, a male and female cardinal land on

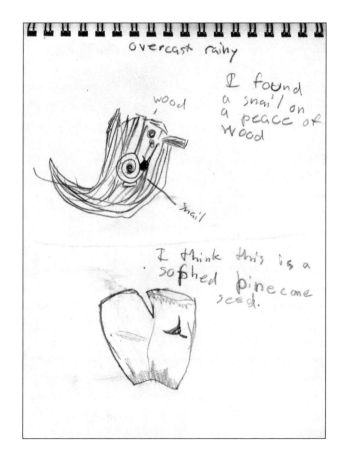

FIGURE 5.6 - When Samantha writes, "I *think* this is a soft pinecone seed," she demonstrates her developing critical thinking skills and wants more evidence before making a conclusive identification.

the feeder and put their beaks together. Jocelyn immediately switches gears and writes: "A male and female cardinal came to the feeder and kissed."

"You are so smart to write that down, Jocelyn. You will never forget this moment!"

In the circle Paige passes her yellow-button-covered leaf.

"What do you infer these are?" I ask the class.

"Eggs."

"Fungus."

"I think it's just a normal leaf because I've seen lots of oak leaves that look like that."

We accept all the ideas and the day ends with Samantha walking around the circle holding a teeny snail shell she found.

Reflections

As I spread out the wet rain ponchos and measuring equipment across the desks, tables, and windowsills after school, I recognize that the study of insect life cycles, a required science curriculum unit, has dovetailed seamlessly with our nature study at the stream. Even though I did not set a focus for our exploration today, my students instinctively transferred a month of observations in a controlled classroom setting to an open-ended investigation in the natural world.

This process of using nature study to teach mandatory science concepts has been building throughout the year. In early October we talked about what a habitat provides—food, water, air, and space—when Sabina brought in a monarch caterpillar to share. She agreed to leave it in our classroom so that we could observe its life cycle.

In November Shaundra found a larva that she presented as a worm. Sabina, with her monarch experience, walked by and announced, "That's a caterpillar." Then, when Shaundra shared her find, it was an opportunity to examine the insect life cycle because I was pretty sure that this early in the year, most of my students had not internalized a larva as a life cycle stage.

"What is the difference between this caterpillar and a worm?" I began.

"It has legs."

"You can tell which end is the head."

"I know birds eat larva."

We passed Shaundra's share around, and when everyone felt sure that indeed it was a larva, I asked, "What will happen next?"

"It will be a butterfly."

"Something else happens first," I prompted.

"A cocoon."

"Or a chrysalis."

"Right, and what is the scientific word that starts with a *p*?"

A joyful chorus of "pupa" followed.

"Right, and if it finds a protective spot, it will stay a pupa all winter long and hatch out into an adult insect in the spring. But we don't know if it will be a beetle or a butterfly or a moth or something else."

When teaching moments occur organically like this, my students are immediately engaged, receptive, and focused.

A similar dynamic worked when teaching a physical science unit on air and weather. One activity involved submerging a vial (with a paper towel stuffed inside) upside down in a tank of water, trying to keep it dry. Lots of conversation was generated about the bubbles formed as the vial went down. For many years I had wondered how best to investigate the bubbles that suddenly take shape in the quick-flowing stream waters after the November rains. Now I had the perfect segue to build on the properties of air trapped in water.

By the time we begin an in-depth study of measurement in late spring, my students have had considerable practical experience at the stream with a variety of tools and units of measure. As we revisit the measurement chart we created at the beginning of the school year in preparation for stream study, my students see weight, capacity, area, and perimeter as logical extensions of how to quantify their world. Likewise, when Jade suggested measuring the robin's egg last month, it was natural for her to bring her measurement experiences at the stream back into the classroom.

Friday, June 3, Lodi, NY

I have just finished filling the tube feeders and was sitting on the deck finishing my breakfast cereal, enjoying the usual gang—goldfinches, purple finches, and house sparrows. I hear a truck stop in front of the house and assume it is Georgie come to mow. Then a black dog comes around the back of the house. The dog and I look at each other, and suddenly the shape of the head and ears do not look quite right. My eyes widen, my mouth forms an "oh, my, it's a bear," and I run inside. The bear heads for the full bird feeders, stands on its hind legs, holds on to the perches of the longer feeder, and sticks its tongue into the holes for black oil sunflower seeds. It pulls harder, bending the feeder pole and then sits down comfortably to continue eating while I take still photos and movies through the closed French doors.

I call the New York State Department of Conservation and talk to Mr. Angotti, who tells me bears can smell food a mile away. I can let the bear finish eating or try to scare it off by hitting pans together. He figures by the size I describe (about five feet long) that it's probably a yearling kicked out of its mother's den. I decide to let the bear finish eating. By now he has knocked the large feeder to the ground and lies stretched out on the grass just below the deck. I look out on a glossy black mass of fur that conjures up the idea of dog and pet rather than dangerous wild animal.

Exactly one hour and fifteen minutes later my visitor stands up on all fours, one more time noses the empty small feeder now hanging about two feet from the ground, sniffs the grass, turns his back to the house, and ambles across the lawn. He stops once to leave steaming proof that he was here and zigzags his way between the two apple trees in the direction of the pond where I hope he takes a long cool drink before heading toward lunch.

TUESDAY, JUNE 8: A YEAR AT THE STREAM

We gather quietly in the circle to begin our last stream study. When I announce that there will be no measurements today everyone cheers, including the parents.

"Let's head out together today and do our best fox walks," I counter in my most enthusiastic voice.

"Can we go to other people's sit spots?" asks Olivia.

"Yes, and start thinking about what you liked most about stream study this year."

Before we get to the woods, Helena picks up a piece of wood and, bubbling over with excitement, exclaims, "Laurie, I think I found evidence of something." She is not ready to make an inference; still I quietly appreciate the language that has become commonplace throughout our day.

We all travel up the stream together and within seconds someone finds a dead blue jay. Instantly blue jay feathers are in everyone's hands.

FIGURE 5.7 - At year's end my students bond as a knowledgeable community of naturalists. They share a sense of ownership and caring about their woods and its creatures.

"Let's remember to wash our hands as soon as we get back to the classroom," I advise, and then stop everyone to examine a tree with many holes in it.

"Woodpecker holes," the cry goes up.

"It's an acorn woodpecker," asserts Samantha, who then quickly corrects herself.

"No, it couldn't be because *they* live in California."

Now the discoveries begin in earnest. Many larvae are found, and no one calls them worms as they did in the fall. Victoria finds a snail that reminds her of our trout-release field trip to Salmon Creek the previous week, where we collected them by the handful. Eric, Luis, and Sydney use pieces of wood to dig into a log they find next to the stream. They are lost in a pretend world where they mine for ore. Daniel picks up a giant rock, then finds and pulls out a two-lined salamander.

Someone else finds a dead salamander and the call goes out to bury it. A group of students collects a pile of wooden twigs and builds a narrow rectangle on the ground. They lay the salamander inside the rectangle and place a flat rock on top of it where they scratch out the words, "Sally Died." When four students decide to say a prayer, they kneel down, putting the palms of their hands together in front of their chests. The words "God" and "peace" rise occasionally out of the soft burble of their individual prayers (see Figure 5.7).

Others go off quietly by themselves. Samantha and Sabina take their nature journals to private spots where they closely observe what is right in front of them. Samantha sits on a log drawing a spider web, complete with resident spider and egg sac. Sabina settles on the ground fascinated by a patch of mayapple plants where something has taken a bite out of a mature fruit.

After forty minutes I gather everyone together for nature journaling at the Chipmunks' sit spot where a log, a bench, and a plot of flat land can accommodate all of us (see Figure 5.8).

FIGURE 5.8 - Some students join me, eager to share their entries, as we write memories of our year at the stream.

"Write about your stream memories over the year," I begin. "It could be a small moment or a poem."

Many students write about their adventures today and four or five write poems (see Figure 5.9).

Nicholas, who still struggles as a writer, sits down next to me, his journal open to a blank page.

"Okay, Nicholas, write down what you remember," I begin, aware that I just want to drink in these last moments of stream study on my own.

Just then Nicholas finds a leaf with a dime-sized lacy pattern.

"What's this, what's this?"

His face lights up, full of expression, not the way it usually is—flat and dulled from the medication he takes for ADHD. I try to explain that if we could peel

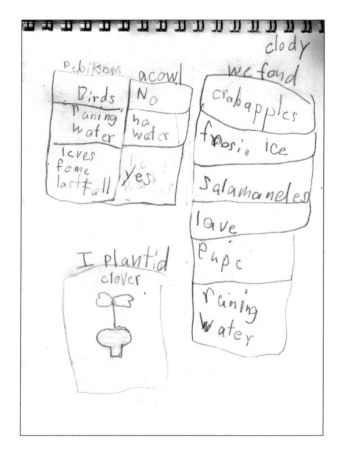

FIGURE 5.9 - Victoria writes her predictions for the day ("birds, running water, leaves from last fall") and what she actually found ("no, no water, yes") followed by a list of her memories.

off the green covering of the leaf, we would see this same lacy pattern covering all of it. He looks at me quizzically.

"Probably an insect ate the leaf and uncovered this pattern."

"Can I draw it?"

"Of course."

Relieved to have a plan, Nicholas carefully outlines the leaf and pencils in a crosshatching of lines to show where the leaf was eaten.

When everyone finishes, we sit on the log stretched across the stream to have our picture taken (see Figure 5.10). The walk back to our classroom is gentle and subdued.

Today I ask everyone to share something. Nicholas makes sure he heard correctly.

"Can we pass?" he asks.

"Not today, Nicholas. I'd like to hear everyone's thoughts about the stream."

When the share comes around to Brie, she says, "Same as Jocelyn."

FIGURE 5.10 - It is a rare and sweet moment when we gather together at the stream site as a whole class.

FIGURE 5.11 - Rainbow guides her pre-K buddy across the dry streambed in early June.

Brie, who joined our class in mid-October, is still shy and uneasy. She often falls asleep at the circle and spends a lot of time in the nurse's office. Earlier today she went to the nurse with a stomachache. I decide to nudge a bit more and ask her to repeat what Jocelyn actually said. When she cannot remember, the rest of the class tries to help.

"Was it the larva Jocelyn found that you wanted to talk about?" asks Luis.

"Yes," she answers, "And also the daddy longlegs."

Those six words are the ribbon around the gift Brie has already given to me. At the stream today, she showed me the list she recorded in her journal of everything she saw. Before she walked away she smiled up at me and said, "Laurie, I don't have a stomachache any more."

Reflections

At first I am taken aback when everyone cheers about no measuring, but I soon realize that we are all, including me, just wanting to get out into the natural world and embrace it, each in our own way.

Every year final stream study day looks a bit different, but it is always a time to celebrate our love of nature and all it has to offer. One year we brought our pre-K buddies to visit the stream, and I watched proudly as my students became natural world ambassadors for their young charges (see Figure 5.11).

Today I ask my students to write about their memories *after* we explore at the stream and I find that most choose to write about what they just experienced. In previous years we wrote our reflections about stream study in the classroom first and then went outside to say good-bye. Those writing sessions generated musings about the whole year of stream visits (see Figures 5.12 and 5.13).

Either way these June nature journal entries provide a snapshot assessment, not only of writing skills but also of my students' connection to the natural world. One year Sophia wrote:

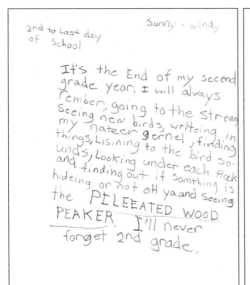
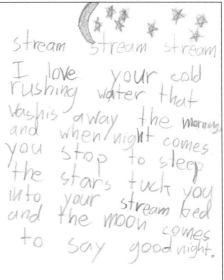

FIGURE 5.12 - FIGURE 5.13 - Prompted to write reflections close to the last day of school, Sophie lists her memories and Elizabeth expresses herself in a poem.

Dear Nature Diary,

The stream was the first place I saw a salamander and crayfish in a stream. My most exciting time at the stream was when we found our first crayfish in the stream.

The Stream

The stream, the stream

The lovely, lovely stream

Where the water glitters

Like diamonds

The beautiful stream

Where I daydream

The stream oh the stream

I love the stream

Jordan expressed a similar sentiment:

It was the first place I've seen a salamander. I've seen so many birds there. And that place is . . . the stream.

Brian, a most challenged learner and a challenging student to teach, was the master of learned helplessness in the classroom, but on this day he wrote a list of his favorite memories completely on his own:

I liked the animals.

I liked the trees.

I liked lifting up the rocks.

I remember the little crayfish.

I remember going in the woods with Mr. Jenson (the school principal).

I remember being quiet going in the woods to listen to birds.

And Lucas shows his appreciation in a short ode entitled "Thank You Stream":

Thank you

Stream

For your

Inhabitants

And life.

Thank you.

I sit down with my students to write a reflection of my own:

This is our last "official" journal entry. The journals have been a fabulous addition and enrichment for stream study. Everyone is writing quietly, independently. Jordan has his home journal next to him with beautiful feathers taped inside. How could I have launched such a successful nature study without Jordan—so enthusiastic, such a great observer. He inspired me so. All of these students, I hope, will always be attuned to their natural world. I certainly hope I don't lose the joy and the wonder of this year.

In fact, there have been students like Jordan and Daniel and Samantha every year—who teach, question, and delight me, and no, I never lost the joy and wonder of that year.

A YEAR AT THE STREAM REVISITED

At Open House, the day before school begins, one or two children present me with a pinecone, a nest, or even a monarch caterpillar contentedly chewing a milkweed leaf inside a plastic container. By the time I meet my new students, word has spread, and these incoming second graders know me as the "nature teacher." As I delight over each gift, pointing out the intricate details, I am ready to embark on another rewarding journey of discovery and exploration.

In *September and October*, as we establish our routines, the natural world is my ally, helping me to engage my students as active learners and to create a classroom community that is inclusive in every sense of the word. After several visits to the stream, even the most tentative students, those who were fearful of open space and yucky worms, begin the daily mantra, "Is it stream study today?" And in an environment where everyone can be successful, my most challenged learners contribute in ways they would not attempt inside the classroom.

Throughout the year I use the discovery and exploration of the natural world to nurture my students' critical thinking skills. It takes time and in *November* my students may still be asking questions, expecting teachers and parents to supply immediate answers. At our classroom window and with our moments of silence at the stream, they are still in training, learning how to stop, think a moment, and try out their own hypotheses.

As we look for signs and evidence of animal activity in *December*, they are developing a practice and habit of careful observation. It is often not until *January* that I begin to notice the profound impact of nature study on my students' thinking and on their lives in and out of the classroom.

One January, as I am about to introduce a study of peacemakers, I decide to ask my students what we have studied so far this year, curious to see what they will say. The first reply, communities, makes sense, for we finished up this social studies unit right before December vacation. Then, in quick succession, they add birds, nature, stream study. Eventually my students remember writing, reading, and math, not realizing how well integrated the "three Rs" have become in our investigations (see Chapters 6 and 7).

I am pleased that nature study is so present and alive in their minds. Their experiences and discoveries in the natural world appear forever internalized when they recall a particular encounter in perfect detail. Seemingly overnight their language is peppered with words such as *observe, identify, infer,* and *hypothesize* during discussions that become more frequent and last longer. We add to our nature lore and begin to solidify scientific concepts introduced early in the year. We begin to tackle questions like, How can you tell which way a rabbit is going? Why does zero mean freezing? How do you determine whether a speed is fast or slow?

By *February* we are so comfortable in the natural world that we view the stream and its surrounding woods as an old friend. We observe, record entries in our journals, and take accurate measurements, but we also laugh, flop in the snow, slide on the ice, and set ourselves free to enjoy the best amusement park in the world.

When the winter snows begin to thaw in *March*, I usually notice a significant increase in the shares that students are bringing in from the natural world. The more I intentionally value the assortment of rocks and sticks and feathers that appear each week, the more my other students begin to search their own backyards, parks, playgrounds, ball fields, and parking lots. Also around this time, as the world starts to turn green again, my students keep a vigilant eye on what is going on outside our classroom window. Somehow we manage to maintain a balance between honoring exciting activity and staying focused on classroom work.

In *April* my students' independence as watchful observers of the natural world is well established. They instinctively use all their senses, not just their sight. Together we begin to synthesize what we have learned. Sometimes it takes the form of a student understanding material well enough to tell a joke, like Jocelyn's remark about an adult darkling beetle being older than a second grader. Or we can examine measurement data gathered throughout the year to understand how scientists use this kind of information to make predictions about the physical world. And in *May* it becomes clear that we are constantly synthesizing our study of scientific concepts in the classroom with our authentic observations in the field.

By the end of the school year, we look for ways to be outside as often as possible. One warm spring day in May, we go outside to release our last painted lady butterfly. We form a circle on the grass behind the school and in front of our classroom window. The butterfly stays in the center when we release it and flies around the circle as if to say good-bye to each of us. At least that is what we think. Just as the butterfly takes off, we all hear the unmistakable call of the pileated woodpecker back in the woods, right at the place where some students spotted it two days earlier during stream study.

Spontaneously, I decide we will walk into the woods to try and find it. No reminders are necessary to walk quietly. The pileated seems to be calling from many different directions. When we reach our destination, everyone sits down, some on a wooden bench, some on a log. We sit, we wait, and we listen. After a while we hear the pileated cry from a long distance and finally, conceding the improbability of a sighting, we return for lunch. But it has been a magical moment—sitting in the woods together, enjoying absolute silence, content to wait for a majestic bird to appear.

In *June*, thanks to a connected parent, we are lucky enough to visit the bird specimen collection at the Cornell Museum of Vertebrates. The museum archives "skins" (complete birds that are preserved for research but not mounted as lifelike taxidermy exhibits) from the smallest hummingbird to the imposing golden eagle. We are thrilled to see not only a pileated woodpecker up close but also its extinct cousin, the ivory-billed woodpecker. Irby Lovette, our guide for the morning, takes me aside to marvel at my students' interest and attention.

"You should be proud of your students, and they should be proud of you. I have never brought such a young group of students to the skin lab who were so knowledgeable."

I am immensely proud and pleased to receive this unexpected affirmation from an expert.

During the last week of school, all the second-grade classes go on a final field trip together to celebrate the move to third grade. In case of rain, we always secure the use of a large pavilion in a city park located at the southern tip of Cayuga Lake. Students spread throughout the park under the watchful eye of teachers and parents. Soccer matches, playground equipment, feeding the ducks, and fishing, as well as indoor crafts and games, offer enough choices for everyone.

After lunch, I ask who wants to go for a nature walk along the lake's shore. This particular year, eleven of my seventeen students (plus two from another class) choose to join me. Four students bring their nature journals and six wear binoculars. On the way, many gull, goose, and mallard feathers are collected, but the most prized are the female mallard feathers adorned with a spot of indigo blue. Christian, an experienced fisherman, identifies every dead fish we see—creek chub, catfish, bullhead, and carp. Damian stops to show me the bird guts he finds on the grass. What I love is everyone's ease in the natural world. They skip along the path, eager to share each new discovery.

When we return, I join five students observing Canada geese in the muddy edges along the lake's shore. We watch birds preening, swimming, sleeping, and fighting. When a few first graders come along from another school, teasing the birds and calling "duckie, duckie, duckie!" my students are indignant.

"Those are Canada geese," Eva remarks dryly, as if to say, "don't you *know* that?"

My students insist on precise language to describe their world. Words such as *evidence*, *inference*, *hypothesis*, and *conclusion* are now part of their daily vocabulary. And like Samantha, they can make an impulsive inference, think it through, and correct themselves.

As in every content area, there is a developmental range among second graders, and how they relate to the natural world varies. Although there are always a few eight-year-olds ready to wander off to sit spots, nature journals in hand, drawing and writing about the changes throughout the seasons, many others would prefer to build dams, collect acorns, or dig for treasure. But it is just this range of students who through the years have sought me out—on the front steps after school to tell me about the red eft in their backyard, at my classroom door to bring me a diorama made entirely of natural materials, or even via e-mail to send me a photo of a crow nesting in a tall Norway spruce. I remain confident that most of my students, no matter how they choose to connect with the natural world as young children, will have cultivated a relationship that will stay with them for the rest of their lives (see Chapter 8).

CHAPTER 6

Literacy Through Nature Study— Reading

One afternoon in February we return from a field trip with just enough time before dismissal to read a chapter in *Poppy* by Avi, a book I return to year after year. We are closing in on the story's resolution as Poppy, a deer mouse, is about to reach New House, the destination she has been struggling toward for many chapters. In the story, Poppy has promised to secure a salt lick for her friend Ereth, a porcupine, in exchange for his protection en route, but she has not yet figured out how to get the salt down to her level. So far my students have predicted that when Poppy arrives at New House she might find an owl, a cat, or a porcupine. Today's reading reveals an owl twice the size of her adversary, the great horned owl Mr. Ocax. As I close the book, most of my students head for the hallway to collect their gear, but Anna is sitting pensively on the rug.

"What are you thinking, Anna?"

"Nothing."

As I give Anna some wait time, Ariella approaches.

"I think [this new] owl will try to eat Poppy and knock over the salt lick and all the pieces will fall on the ground."

Anna has been listening to Ariella and decides it is now safe enough to reveal her thinking after all.

"I think it's not a real owl. They have those owls around to scare away the birds. I've seen them."

As Anna and Ariella walk out together continuing their literary conversation, I sit rooted, smiling with pride. Both girls will soon find their inferences validated. Rarely, in over ten years of reading this novel, have students made such accurate inferences, let alone two in a row. It is a stunning moment. Are my students learning to be keen observers of their inner and outer worlds, I wonder? Is their awareness of the natural world supporting their ability to activate their metacognition? In our discussions about Avi's characters we have noted that, although they talk like people, in other ways Avi uses the characteristics of real wild animals to move the plot forward. For example, porcupines *do* love salt and live solitary lives as adults. Thus Ereth is portrayed as a curmudgeon who starts drooling at the mere thought of a salty snack. My diagnostic wheels are still spinning as Joey comes back into the classroom.

"I think it's an eagle owl because they are much bigger than great horned owls."

Yes, I think, there *is* something going on here. I will be on the lookout for more connections between nature study and the other learning behaviors I try to foster in my classroom.

As I walk my class to the buses, I continue to ponder the increase in my students' metacognitive behavior after six years of placing nature study at the core of my teaching. Do the observations we make in the natural world, the emphasis on critical thinking skills, the moments of science, and the reading comprehension strategies we study all merge together to support children's thinking as I read aloud?

On that day, energized by these possibilities, I start using a digital recorder to keep an oral account of how my students' literary lives dovetail with their appreciation of the natural world. On that day, this chapter is born.

❋ ❋ ❋

As children become naturalists, as they strive to understand the world they live in, as they learn to observe, ask questions, make hypotheses, and look for evidence in the natural world, they are also rehearsing essential comprehension strategies that will enhance their literary lives. Throughout the school year as we work on making connections and inferences, asking questions, visualizing, and determining importance while we read, the natural world provides us with multiple opportunities to develop the language of metacognition.

We *connect* one experience to another—a salamander reminds us of the time we found three of the same species under one rock. We use a pile of scat to *infer* which animal may have been under a particular tree. We constantly ask the *question*—what happened here? And as we try to answer, we *visualize* that event in our minds. Often we begin a stream visit by standing silently for a minute, becoming aware of all of our senses as we look, listen, smell, and touch. We also *determine* which features are *important* to look for when trying to identify a new bird.

While we are rehearsing metacognitive language at our stream, back in the classroom I use read-alouds, following the model detailed in Ellin Keene's *Mosaic of Thought* (Keene and Zimmerman 2007), to demonstrate how to notice what you are thinking in the midst of reading. Thus I explain to my students that when I stop reading and look toward the ceiling, I am sharing my internal thoughts out loud. It takes the entire school year to teach all five strategies, but during that time I make sure that we are constantly revisiting and practicing the ones previously introduced. As I begin to teach inferences, for example, my students are working toward mastery on making connections. I find it helpful to choose a specific content area in social studies or science, a different literary genre when possible, and a predetermined time frame to introduce each comprehension strategy.

Making Connections: We start off the school year with a focus on stream study. My students find many ways to *connect* their new experiences in the natural world when I read fictional stories set in the forest or near a stream. Sometimes the connection works in reverse when a student references a fact learned from nonfiction text while we are outside.

Making Inferences: Right after Thanksgiving vacation, we launch a second-grade social studies unit about community. We look for clues to *infer* the difference between urban, suburban, and rural communities in picture books and through images in the computer lab.

Questioning: In January a study of peacemakers generates thinking *questions* that do not always have an obvious answer. My students ask, "Why do so many peacemakers like Martin Luther King, Jr., Gandhi, or Harvey Milk get killed? Why did white people hate black people? How did peacemakers have the courage to do what they did?" As we read about peacemakers around the world and throughout history, we also discover the common features of biography.

Visualizing: Although we read and memorize poems all year long, during the months of March and April we write poetry, examine how poets evoke all five senses, and, as we notice the pictures forming in our minds, learn how to *visualize*.

Determining Importance: We end the school year reading and writing nonfiction text. After reading a page, a section, or a chapter providing factual information, we brainstorm what we think is most *important* to remember. Then we apply this skill when we are *writing* nonfiction to make sure the essential facts are included.

MAKING CONNECTIONS

I reserve the first six weeks of school for establishing reading routines, using character study to introduce the range of book series in our classroom library, and teaching my students how to choose a "just-right" book to read. Although I wait until mid-October to formally introduce *making connections*, my students are jumping up and down with "reminds me of" comments when I read *Crawdad Creek* by Scott Russell Sanders early in September because the connection to our own stream experience is unmistakable. *The Salamander Room* by Anne Mazer (1991) takes us back to the many northern two-lined and northern red-backed salamanders we have found together.

By the time I read *The Raft* by Jim LaMarche (2002) and ask the question, "What are you thinking?" my students are already instinctively using many of the comprehension strategies we will study. (*The Raft* is the story of a young boy not wanting to spend the summer with his grandmother because she has no television. In the end, he jumps into numerous adventures and makes a strong connection to the natural world.)

Together Eric and Luis are beside themselves with the *inference* that grandma, knowing Nickie is bored, puts the raft in his path so he will have something to do. As we go around the circle making comments at the end of the story, many *connections* are made to my students' personal experiences. Jade establishes herself as a reader who asks *questions*. "Who really put the raft there?" she still wonders. Samantha comments on Nickie's bravery, going into the mud to rescue the fawn. Paige points out how Nickie changed from the beginning to the end of the book.

This merging of comprehension strategies and nature study is a recurrent dynamic in my classroom. We are well on our way, metacognitively speaking, by the time I use *The Other Way to Listen* by Byrd Baylor (1997) to model how to make text-to-self connections.

"Byrd Baylor is one of my favorite authors because all of her stories take place in the natural world."

I begin to read and stop at these pages to demonstrate my thinking:

On the first page the old man says, "It takes lots of practice. You can't be in a hurry."

I'm thinking about when I was a little girl and I became frustrated learning how to ride a two-wheeler and my parents told me, "You have to practice."

About thirteen pages from the end the old man says, "Do this: go get to know one thing as well as you can."

That's just what I like to do in the natural world.

About six pages from the end the girl finds hawk feathers.

I remember how excited I was when I found my first turkey tail feather with stripes on it.

When I finish reading, we go around the circle and many students share the obvious—feathers they found or the rocky side of a hill they were sitting on. Then Jade says, "This is going to be weird but I *feel* something. It's reminding me about something I *feel*, but it didn't really happen to me." Jade is trying to explain that the feeling of the book is familiar but not a particular incident in the book. When the share makes its way to Luis, he says, "same as Jade." As their teacher, I am humbled by their insightful and unexpected connection.

I teach the term *text-to-self connection* and then ask the deeper question encouraged in the second edition of *Mosaic of Thought*: "When you make a connection like this, how does it help you understand the story better?"

"When you make a connection, then you remember something in your life," Paige suggests.

Other responses continue to talk around the question until Samantha shares, "Well when he was leaning against a tree, it was like when I lean against my dog."

"What does it feel like when you lean against your dog?"

Samantha adds, "Well my dog respects me, and I respect my dog?" She is remembering the old man's advice (from *The Other Way to Listen*) to "respect that tree or hill or whatever it is you're with."

"But what is the *feeling* that you have? As you describe it to us, it sounds kind of calm and peaceful."

When Samantha nods in agreement, I turn to my class.

"Samantha understands how the old man was feeling, leaning against the tree, calm and peaceful, because that's just the way she feels leaning on her dog."

The next day we repeat the routine with *Where the River Begins* by Thomas Locker (1984). When I come to the page where Josh and Aaron are jumping across the river with their grandfather, I share connections, but this time I also explain how they help me understand the story better.

I remember jumping rocks in an Adirondack river—it was really fun but also scary because I was afraid that I might slip—my experience helps me understand how the kids in the story might be feeling.

I also remember the icy cold water so I can imagine how cold the kids' feet must be—it helps me feel like I am right there with them.

Today when I close the book, we only have time for a few connections, but when Luis remembers being in a tent and staying dry, I try to involve the whole class.

"Who else has a camping connection?" Many hands go up.

"Who can tell how it helped to understand the story better?"

The idea of moving beyond a simple connection—it reminds me of—to articulating how it helps understand a story better, is a new skill for my students. So when they report a connection, I model language to nudge them toward this new way of thinking.

"I remember being in a hot sleeping bag."

"So, like Luis, you can understand how cozy, warm, and safe the children feel."

"I remember roasting marshmallows on a stick."

"So you can imagine the warmth of the fire on their faces and the soft mushy insides of the marshmallows."

"My mom used to tell scary stories at night around the campfire."

"So it's as if you're right there in the story, sitting between Josh and Aaron, listening to their grandfather."

"I can hear the river singing just like in the other story, *The Other Way to Listen*."

With this comment, Jade helps me introduce *text-to-text connections*.

"Jade, the singing river in Byrd Baylor's book helped you hear the river in this book."

As I conference with individual students during independent reading time over the next few weeks, I will ask for connections (text-to-self and text-to-text). I celebrate every connection, and, if a student is willing to share with the whole class, we take a minute to rehearse together. Sharing aloud two or three days a week is enough to keep the momentum going and keep the practice of noticing connections fresh. I respond in the same way when we go to our stream site:

"When I go to Nicholas's house, he has a stream just like this one."

"So you're making a connection between our stream and Nicholas's stream. You are noticing your thinking. Good for you!"

"I learned how to find salamanders at camp."

"Oh! So that's why you're picking up rocks? You just made a connection between your salamander hunts at camp and finding a salamander right now."

Much later in the year, I am reading the February chapter in *Walk When the Moon Is Full* by Frances Hammerstrom (1975). When I get to the part describing the willow branches bent down so close to the ice that the rabbits can eat them, Victoria raises her hand and tries to explain a text-to-text connection she is making. She cannot remember the book title, but after several tries, with other students joining in, they collectively make a connection to the ice storm that breaks all the tree limbs in *Gooseberry Park* by Cynthia Rylant. I explain that the willow tree in Hammerstrom's book is young and so its branches are flexible enough to bend under the weight of the ice. In *Gooseberry Park*, many of the trees were old and their brittle branches broke easily in the ice storm, including the pin oak where Stumpy the squirrel had her nest.

As I inwardly celebrate this moment, my students revel in Hammerstrom's conclusion when the children take their grandmother to look at the tree branches and ask *her* to infer what could have chewed the branches up so high. Grandma says, "Squirrels, of course." Her grandchildren exclaim, "Fooled you, fooled you, it was a rabbit."

MAKING INFERENCES

In mid-November I launch our study of community and use *The Little House* by Virginia Lee Burton (1969) to introduce *inference*. We use the pictures as evidence to determine the difference between urban, rural, and suburban neighborhoods. It is obvious that the little house starts out in the countryside. As the story continues, I stop to make a few predictions, a type of inference already familiar to my students:

I am inferring that a city is going to be built around the little house because there are so many houses on this page.

I am inferring that the little house won't like the city because she misses the hills of daisies.

I read *The House on Maple Street* by Bonnie Pryor and Beth Peck (1992) next because I know it will not only solidify the features of different communities but will also give my students many opportunities to make text-to-text connections with *The Little House*. In fact, we start out slowly when, about halfway through *The House on Maple Street*, students make connections and eventually one or two try an inference.

"The stream is like our stream. It's in the woods."

"This story is reminding me of *The Little House* because it starts in the country and now it's a town."

"It's like *The Little House*. First there are horses and carriages and now there are old-fashioned cars."

"I think some kids are going to find that lost cup and arrowhead at the end of the book."

"I think the kids at the beginning of the story will be at the end."

By the time I read *The Paperboy* by Dav Pilkey (1999), most of my students are fluent in the language of communities. We have practiced with several read-alouds and also with black and white community images in the computer lab where we worked in partners to answer the question, "What do you infer (urban, suburban, or rural) and what is the clue in the photo to support your inference?"

In no time we infer that all three neighborhoods are represented in Pilkey's story: The factory and the newspaper warehouse indicate urban. As the newspaper truck follows its route, the fields and houses suggest a rural locale. Finally, the paperboy delivers his newspapers on a block with houses, lawns, and driveways that could be suburban.

We finish the story, and, on the way to lunch, Daniel, already an accomplished birder and always thoughtful about his world, tells me that he notices woodpeckers are always on the suet and other birds are not. I waste no time asking him what he might infer.

"That the woodpecker likes that food, I guess."

"Sounds good to me," I say as we smile at each other.

When Mia spots a new bird, a downy woodpecker, on the feeder after recess, I repeat Daniel's inference and then add one of my own.

"I infer that woodpeckers might like suet because it is similar to what they eat in the natural world. What *do* woodpeckers eat?"

We have a short discussion that concludes when Samantha explains, "The larvae [that woodpeckers eat] have a lot of fat that gives them energy and the suet is made of fat, that's what clumps it together." We soon begin our math lesson, and, once again, I appreciate the power of the natural world to help us strengthen our metacognitive muscles.

In early December I read Lindsay Barrett George's *In the Woods: Who's Been Here?* (1998) before we go out to the stream. Instead of talking about signs or clues, I use the language of inference and evidence.

"Let's look at the pictures and see what inferences we can make."

"Who's been here?" I read as we examine the first illustration of a nest.

My students are eager to get started. They infer bird, robin, and squirrel. On the next page something hangs from a milkweed leaf and everyone agrees it's a monarch caterpillar.

"What was the evidence that helped you infer this would be a monarch caterpillar?"

"Monarchs like to eat milkweed."

The last page I read today shows blue feathers. Every hand flies up in the air. Blue jay and bluebird are the guesses so my students are surprised to see a goshawk and a dead blue jay on the next page. Luis remembers that Dr. Evans, a guest scientist, taught us that birds are always losing feathers but just a few at a time since they need them to fly. We now realize there were too many feathers in the picture for just normal wear and tear and will be more cautious about our inferences when we go outside today (see Figure 6.1).

How to Be a Nature Detective by Millicent E. Selsam (1995) (also published as *Big Tracks, Little Tracks*) is another surefire hit in my classroom and lends itself to practicing inference. The first mystery to solve is which animal ate the dog food and the cat food. Sydney points out some important evidence that no one, not even I, has ever noticed before in all the years I have read this book.

"Look," she explains. "The ball of yarn and the mouse toy are next to the dog bowl and the ball, squeeze toy, and sneaker are next to the cat bowl. My dog loves to chew shoes so I think the dog ate the cat food and the cat ate the dog food."

"Great detective work, Sydney. Those clues support your inference."

I try to use the language of inference whenever possible. After the first big snow, we look at the tracks outside our window, think about the animals we usually see, and infer which animals may have passed by. Whenever we note the features and behaviors of a new bird at the feeder, we look for evidence to infer the bird's identity. In March Daniel brings in the remnants of an owl pellet in a plastic ziplock bag. As he finishes his share, Samantha's hand waves frantically, threatening to break off at the wrist.

FIGURE 6.1 - Miryam uses abbreviations to record her inferences about the tracks she found near the stream—raccoon, rabbit, deer, human, unknown, and squirrel.

"I'd like to make a prediction about something in the bag. I saw a pointy orange bone, and I want to estimate—no, *predict*—that the owl ate a bird."

"Samantha was right to change her idea from an estimate to a prediction, but Samantha, what you actually did is make an inference: you used a clue in the bag—the pointy orange bone—to infer that the owl might have eaten a bird."

When I take a closer look, I realize that the pointy bone is a curved orange tooth. I decide to explain that rodents are constantly chewing and gnawing and that this is probably one of the front incisors that continues to grow. Samantha changes her inference to mouse, and I congratulate my students for the smart inferences they are making, not only in books but also in the natural world.

QUESTIONING

"How long do juncos live, Laurie? Actually, how long do all birds live?" Daniel asks when we return from our December vacation.

"I really don't know the answer to that question, Daniel, but I *do* know whom we can ask."

Each year when my students start asking questions about birds, we make a list on chart paper, and later, during a choice time or a visit to the library computer lab, I pull students aside one at a time to type their questions and send an e-mail to Anne Hobbs, the Cornell Lab of Ornithology's public information specialist.

"Laurie, is that a thin question or a thick question?"

Daniel is referring to our latest reading comprehension strategy—questioning. Each year I introduce this strategy during our study of peacemakers, whom we define as people working to make the world a better place. As we read biographies about Martin Luther King, Jr., Mahatma Gandhi, Rachel Carson, Cesar Chavez, Harvey Milk, Wangari Maathai, and others, we share the questions that pop into our minds. Since questioning comes naturally to young children, we focus on making our questions more insightful and discerning. Our *thin questions* clarify information and ideas and often have only one correct answer, revealed later in the book or answered by checking other sources. Our *thick questions*, or thinking questions, ponder more universal ideas and can have many answers or none at all.

For example, while reading *Gandhi* by Demi (2001), our thin questions look for specific information: Did everyone wear *kadhi*, the homespun cloth? What does *defiant* mean? Did the man that killed Gandhi go to jail? Our thick questions are more reflective and take us beyond the text: How did Gandhi (and all peacemakers) decide to become a peacemaker? Is one peacemaker better than another? How do peacemakers stand up and talk in front of so many people? Who was the first peacemaker?

As we develop our ability to question, we move easily between the literary and natural worlds we inhabit. In March, when Rachel asks, "How do birds crack open seeds with their beaks?" I bring this question to the class. We listen to several general responses before Joey demonstrates his keen observation skills.

"I've seen tufted titmice hold a seed between their feet and peck at it."

By May, when hypothesizing and asking questions have become second nature, a spontaneous conversation begins when Luke brings in a deer skull and bones.

"How do you know they are deer bones?" asks Laura.

"My dad told me."

"Were the bones in a pile?" Peter wants to know.

"Yes."

"I think a fox might have come, killed the deer, eaten it, and left the bones," suggests Andres.

"It might have been a bird of prey," proposes Rachel, who is working on a nonfiction book about owls, hawks, and eagles.

"Maybe a hunter came and shot it and left the bones there," is Ariella's contribution.

"I think a python came, swallowed the deer whole, ate it, and then left the bones," comes emphatically from Joey, our resident snake expert.

"Joey, where do pythons live?" I cannot help interjecting at this point.

"The jungle?"

"So do we have the right habitat for pythons?"

"No. But maybe somebody's pet python got out and killed the deer."

"Okay, Joey, is that probable, possible, or unlikely?"

"Possible."

I shrug my shoulders in mock defeat but not without marking the moment, recognizing that my students no longer accept information mechanically. They are thinking for themselves, asking critical questions, and taking risks as they make sense of their internal and external experience.

VISUALIZING

When we begin writing poetry in March, my students have already recited (and many have memorized) over a dozen poems together. The very first poems I introduce are about poems themselves—"Things" by Eloise Greenfield, "A Poem in My Pocket" by Beatrice Schenk de Regniers, and "How to Eat a Poem" by Eve Merriam. Then we continue with poems that connect to our units of study in science and social studies. After reading a poem aloud two times, I simply ask, "What pictures did you see in your mind?" I can usually rely on the same five or six students to raise their hands and make connections about personal experiences—vacations, pets, friends, or families. But a few years into stream study, I notice that a more diverse group of students begin to participate in this exercise.

When I read the last words of "Bridge" by Kristine O'Connell George—"it's a wet and mossy, often soggy crossing" (1998, 14)—almost every hand flies into the air.

"I see the log across our stream."

"Me too."

"Me too!"

"To Walk in Warm Rain" by David McCord reminds everyone of the day we walked to the stream in a light drizzle. With a little prompting we remember the smell of the air, the feel of rain on our faces, and the sound of rain falling through the trees. We unite in a group smile at the end of "Autumn," another O'Connell George favorite, as we point to the collection of dazzling red, orange, and yellow leaves on our display table. Sometimes it works the other way around, when the natural world reminds us of a poem.

One autumn morning during writing workshop, Olivia looks out the window reciting, "the leaves are dancing in the trees," from "Rock and Roll" by Anna Grossnickle Hines (2001). In winter, when the temperature drops and snow begins to pile up in the woods, Luis evokes "The Winter Tree" by Douglas Florian: "she dreams in reams of snow knee-deep" (1999, 21). At the stream many students remark on the abundance of "winter's teeth," from Florian's "Icicles," hanging over the rocks where miniature waterfalls used to tumble (see Figure 6.2).

When we begin a more formal study of visualizing, I use the natural world to give my students multiple sensory experiences because it is impossible to visualize a sunset if you have never seen one or to hear the rustle of leaves on a windy day if you have never stopped to listen. Therefore, in the months leading up to a focus on visualization, I use our first minute of silence at the stream

FIGURE 6.2 - Samantha remembers Douglas Florian's poem and copies it into her nature journal.

to watch the fast-moving clouds, listen for birdsong, smell the crushed leaves under our feet, feel the bark of two different trees, or taste a bit of freshly fallen snow (see Figure 6.3). These experiences help my students visualize as they read independently. When they begin to write poems, elements of the natural world throughout the season—colorful leaves, the sparkle of snowflakes, songbirds landing in a tree, or flowers blooming—become favorite topics they return to because they are safe and familiar (see Appendix B).

In March, blizzard season in upstate New York, we read about the famous blizzard of 1888 in New York City, described in two different children's books— *The Snow Walker* by Margaret K. and Charles Wetterer (1996) and *Anna, Grandpa, and the Big Storm* by Carla Stevens (1998). (*The Day of the Blizzard* by Marietta D. Moskin is another excellent book that could be used with more mature readers.) My students relate to the simple descriptive language used in these books to describe a cold wintry day—*Snow Walker*: "drifts were as hard as icebergs" (14); "gusts of wind scooped up fallen snow" (14); "toes felt icy" (40); *Anna*: "her pompom looked like a big white snowball" (24); "pricking her face like sharp needles" (16); "a blast of icy cold air" (39). Experiences at a winter stream—stomping through snow drifts and getting snow in their boots, sliding

FIGURE 6.3 - My journal entries are a mix of personal observations and anecdotal records about my students. In this March entry I jot down the sounds my students hear during our minute of silence.

FIGURE 6.4 - Charlotte and Emily set up a key where *v key = visualizing* and use their initials to specify who experienced each visualization: *v-ec feel coldness of ice box; v-e feel wind/cold.*

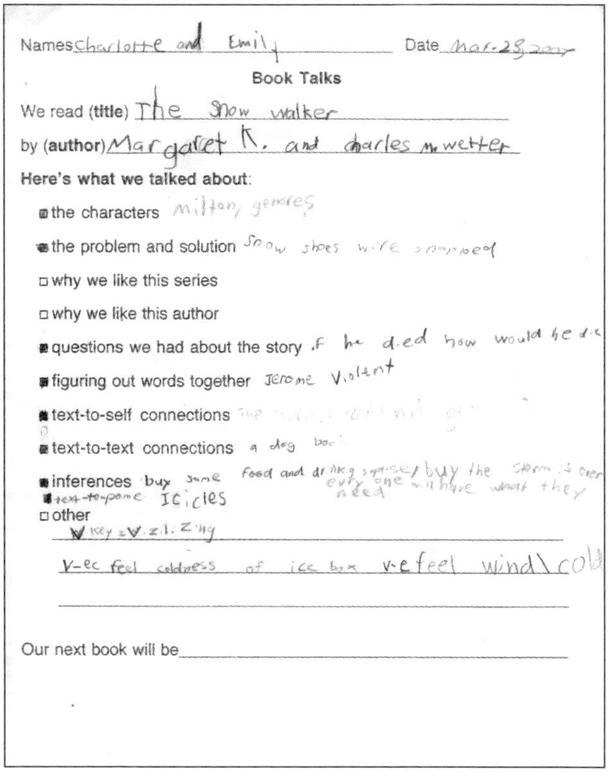
Names Charlotte and Emily Date Mar. 28 2007

Book Talks

We read (title) The Snow walker

by (author) Margaret K. and charles m. wetter

Here's what we talked about:

- the characters milton, genores
- the problem and solution Snow shoes were snapped
- why we like this series
- why we like this author
- questions we had about the story if he died how would he die
- figuring out words together Jerome Violent
- text-to-self connections
- text-to-text connections a dog book
- inferences buy some food and drinks supplies buy the storm is over every one will have what they need
- ~~text-to-pome~~ Icicles
- other

V key = V.z.l. z.ing

V-ec feel coldness of ice box v-e feel wind\cold

Our next book will be

on frozen ice, icy fingers, running noses, and so on—offer my students an entry point to the community of readers who visualize.

I allow my students to choose the book they would like to read for this study, but I always assign their partners, taking into consideration both personality and reading ability. Since neither book qualifies as an easy reader, on occasion I will need to switch a beginning reader from *Anna* to *Snow Walker* (less text and more picture-supported), pairing that student with a more advanced reader. Thanks to enough multiple copies in our school library, most students get their choice and, as a result, are eager to start reading.

After completing an assigned number of pages or chapters, partners are responsible for noticing all the comprehension strategies they use, including visualizations, and for recording them (see Figure 6.4).

They also follow up with a book talk, which might sound something like this, after reading a portion of *Snow Walker*:

Partner #1: I visualized how cold it was.

Partner #2: Which words helped you visualize?

Partner #1 (reading from the text*): "Still, as he pushed through the waves of snow, icy bits blew in. They stung his nose and cheeks."*

Partner #2: How does that help you understand the story?

Partner #1: Well, it made me realize how brave Milton was because he kept helping people even when he was freezing.

As I walk around, conferencing with partners, I am pleased if my students have simply managed to identify descriptive language. Then I consider it my job to facilitate the next step, helping them understand how visualization can enhance their comprehension of the story.

DETERMINING IMPORTANCE

Determining importance is the last comprehension strategy we study, and I do not introduce the term until mid-April when we examine nonfiction as a genre. However, the idea of being mindful when reading text with factual information comes up early in the year as we read about the natural world.

In October I read *Life Cycle of an Oak Tree* by Angela Royston (2003) a few days before we will head to the stream to meet our trees. The text is dense with many unfamiliar terms such as *sapling, catkins,* and *simple* and *compound leaves.* Halfway through I stop reading, assume a quizzical look on my face, a confidential tone, and, as if it had just occurred to me, lean forward to share my thoughts.

"You know, when I read a nonfiction book, there is so much information. It's hard for me to remember it all. As you go back to the circle on the rug please think of one new fact you just learned that you want to remember or a fact you already knew that is especially important to you."

Most of my students say *catkins.* They have never heard this term before, and for now it is enough for them to know that catkins are the flowers of the oak tree. More important, I have planted a seed that I will continue to nourish over time as I remind my students to be attentive readers of nonfiction.

The nonfiction collection makes up a third of my classroom library. There are baskets filled with field guides, animal books, biographies, and a mix of other topics in social studies and science. Titles from such series as Sunshine Reader, Rookie Read-About Science, All Aboard Science, Let's-Read-and-Find-Out Science Book, Step into Reading, DK Eyewitness Readers, First Step Nonfiction, I Can Read, and Heinemann First Library are mixed in with more complex picture books. Throughout the year many students will go through phases of reading nonfiction at home for several weeks at a time. Given the opportunity to choose, students gravitate toward what interests them.

In January, a few months into our bird study, Eric kneels down on the rug to sign in a book he borrowed from the classroom library entitled *How Birds Live*, a Sunshine Reader book. When I ask him to share something he learned, he opens instead to a page with an illustration of a woodpecker.

"Do you know what this is, Laurie, because they don't say?"

"I've never seen that one before, Eric. I wonder if the illustration is accurate."

We walk over to our field guide collection on the windowsill, choose a book of birds from around the world, and find that the red-spotted woodpecker, native to Europe and Asia, has very different markings from the hairy or red-bellied woodpeckers we know. Eric shares his discovery with the class and the revelation that only some of the world's woodpeckers live in North America.

"Eric is a very smart reader of nonfiction," I point out. "He chose a book about birds because he wanted to learn more about them. And when he had a question about a bird he couldn't identify, he used a field guide to get more information."

Particularly captivated by our bird study, Eric will work his way through our collection of bird books and by April feel like enough of an expert to write a chapter book about birds.

In May I require all my students to read nonfiction both at home and in the classroom. Since most of my students choose to read about animals, I have developed over time a large collection of animal books in my classroom library, with special attention to picture-supported simple text.

We begin by identifying and using the features of a nonfiction book to help us understand and learn from the text. Tables of contents, chapter titles, section headings, bold words, captions, maps, diagrams, and illustrations become our comprehension tools. Then we move on to the challenge of identifying the "big idea" of a chapter or a short book. Together we establish big ideas during read-alouds, and I model the use of a graphic organizer where *im-*

portant facts, the big ideas, and *interesting facts*, often examples of the big ideas, can be recorded.

Shortly after the silkworm eggs arrive in our classroom in May, I read *Silkworms* by Donna Schaffer, part of a series on life cycles published by Bridgestone Books. I pause after each page-long section and ask, "What is the most important fact you want to remember?" Our conversation after reading about *larvas* (I substitute the Latin plural *larvae*) goes something like this.

"What do you think is the most important fact to remember about silkworm larvae?"

"They have exoskeletons for protection." (Often students offer the very last fact they hear.)

"They have to eat twenty-four hours after hatching." (Numbers convey significance to many students.)

"They eat mulberry leaves so we need to get some." (This student is thinking critically for sure!)

"They're called silkworms because the larvae look like worms." (I make a mental note to identify this one as an interesting fact.)

At this point my students have identified all four facts included in the larvae section, so I move toward closure.

"You were very good listeners. You remembered all the facts about silkworm larvae in this section. Now, which one tells most about the life of a silkworm larva?"

"Their exoskeletons protect them."

"You are absolutely correct that exoskeletons are important, but what is the author mostly teaching us about in this section?"

"It sounds like they eat a lot of mulberry leaves."

"Yes, and I also remember that the author writes, 'Larvae continue to eat and grow.' How about if we combine that with the mulberry leaves? Is everyone okay with, *Silkworm larvae eat a lot of mulberry leaves and continue to grow?*"

With a show of hands my students agree to my suggestions for an important and then an interesting fact. I add the silkworm facts to the growing list gathered from read-alouds and students' independent reading.

IMPORTANT	INTERESTING
Animals use camouflage for protection.	Chameleons can change color.
Flowers help plants reproduce by making seeds.	When we eat broccoli, we are eating flower buds.
Most birds lay their eggs in nests.	The male emperor penguin puts one egg on his feet under his feathers.
Silkworm larvae eat a lot of mulberry leaves and continue to grow.	Silkworm larvae look like thin worms and that's how they got their name.

I see my role as facilitator in this process, recognizing that it is often more challenging to determine importance in simple text where many small facts seem to have equal weight. With practice many of my students will become more discriminating in their choices for important facts while others will continue to need guidance. Since all my students could use more practice, I also encourage parents to use the same procedure we use in the classroom. In my weekly newsletter home, I write:

Close the book after each chapter (or 5–6 pages) to "stop and think." If your child does not remember what he or she has just read, read it again together. Remind your child that when you read nonfiction, you read more slowly than fiction.

My students have been listening to me read nonfiction text with rapt attention since September, eager to learn about the natural world. By the end of the year, they become part of a vibrant community of readers where everyone is a teacher. The excitement in the room is palpable as students like Eric, eager to share what they have learned on their own, delight us with new insights about inhabitants of the natural world: owls have good hearing; skunks "dance" before they hunt; racoons live in trees.

❋   ❋   ❋

One sunny morning in June, I drop my backpack on my desk and walk right over to the whiteboard to compose a morning message: *What did you learn in second grade? What will you remember from second grade?*

With only two weeks of school left to go, I look for ways to bring closure to our year together. As my students arrive two and three at a time, they walk up to the board, read the questions and write their answers—"birds, insects, math, reading, art" and then someone adds "metacognition," most likely copied from the poster nearby. Later that morning, many students choose to include "metacognition" as they complete a second-grade memories page. Laura even adds, in parentheses, "thinking about my thinking."

In fact, this is gravy time. Recently our book discussions appear to take on a life of their own—exhilarating and rich in metacognitive language. My students, who have always been eager to share their own ideas and move on, are really listening to one another now, responding and building on one another's ideas.

When I read *Crow Call* by Lois Lowry (2009), the discussion that follows becomes an excellent assessment of what my students have internalized about comprehension strategies by the end of the year. Based on real details from Lowry's life, the story involves a little girl who, with some trepidation, goes hunting for crows with her father, just returned from the war. On page 2, the little girl sits "shyly in the front seat of the car next to the stranger who is my father." Four short sentences later we find out that her father has been gone for a long time. I pause and we realize that we were all wondering why she called her father a stranger, and we are pleased that our question is quickly answered. On the next page we wonder why her father says, "having that shirt will help." We soon find out the special history of her oversized plaid shirt, a gift from her father. Daniel raises his hand.

"It's like a pattern, Laurie. A question and then an answer, a question and an answer."

Near the end of the book, after the little girl uses the crow call, a two-page illustration reveals, for the first time, a hundred crows flying through the sky to land in the bare trees and Paige says, "I'm wondering why the father didn't shoot any of the crows."

"Does anyone have an inference?" I ask.

"He won't shoot them because his little girl is worried that the babies won't have parents."

"He wanted the little girl to be happy."

"He was never going to shoot the crows. He just wanted some alone time with his daughter."

My delight in listening to the rich, complex insights of my students is equal to their wonder when I turn to the black and white photo of Lois Lowry on the last page wearing the plaid shirt featured in the book.

"It really happened!" whispers Hannah, her eyes soft with emotion.

A few weeks later, I am looking for a short book and choose *Dot and Jabber and the Mystery of the Missing Stream* by Ellen Stoll Walsh (2002). It opens with two mice trying to figure out why the water in a stream disappears. I scan it quickly, decide it looks engaging, and anticipate that it will elicit connections to our own very dry streambed.

"What are you thinking?" I ask as I show the cover.

"The creek has dried up."

"Only mud will be left."

Pleased that background knowledge is active and flourishing, I affirm my students' inferences and begin to read.

"The detectives couldn't believe their eyes. Leaves and branches were everywhere. 'There is no mystery about this mess,' said Dot. 'The storm last night nearly blew me away.'"

"These detectives are really thinking like scientists," I muse. "They find something. They ask the question, 'Why are all these leaves and branches here?' and they figure out that it is because of the storm."

I continue reading without interruption, close the book, and ask for comments and questions. First we spend a few minutes helping Hannah understand which mouse is Dot and which is Jabber. One after another student offers evidence to prove that Jabber is the tan mouse and Dot the brown one. Next a succession of waving hands shares text-to-text connections with *Poppy and Rye* by Avi, another story of mice, a river, and a dam.

In the middle of the discussion, our reading teacher walks in. She listens for a while and wonders about the beaver dam in one of the illustrations. My students explain that this is not a beaver dam but rather leaves and branches piled up after a rainstorm. They are visualizing the same phenomenon they witnessed in February, when the winter snows melted, turning our gentle stream into a rushing river. They also point out from experience that the continuing rush of water in Dot and Jabber's stream eventually breaks up the dam of piled up leaves.

My short read-aloud turns into a long, involved discussion because my students have been accumulating background knowledge about streams all year. If I had read this story at the beginning of the year, this lively conversation would not have happened. I remind myself that it takes time and practice for a dynamic dialogue like this one to develop. I recognize the importance of continuing to use the language of comprehension strategies—connection, inference, questioning, visualizing, and determining importance—after the terms are introduced. I need to be vigilant, learn to activate the metacognitive "hairs" on the back of *my* neck, and use metacognitive language not only when we are responding to a book but also when we are listening to an announcement on the loudspeaker, solving a math problem, doing a science experiment, walking down the hall, or exploring along our stream.

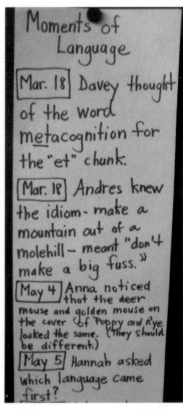

FIGURE 6.5 - Moments of Language are posted next to Moments of Science on the chalkboard.

MOMENTS OF LANGUAGE

In retrospect, it was predictable that one day we would post "Moments of Language" next to the growing list of "Moments of Science." In fact, the very word *metacognition* will take us on a surprising journey where critical thinking skills, moments of science, and reading comprehension strategies continue to merge.

The day I began to value and promote critical thinking skills in my classroom, a profusion of opinions, thoughts, considerations, and evaluations was set free. Not only were my students asking questions, making observations, and trying out new ideas all day long, I had become sensitized to recognizing those moments and taking the time to stop and appreciate them. So moments of language materialized one morning in March as we were brainstorming words with the "-et" chunk.

One by one my students offered their examples—bet, set, let, net, and so on—until Davey, with the tiniest of smirks, offered "metacognition." In his visual search around the classroom, his eyes had found the chart listing our reading strategies under the title "metacognition." Surprised and delighted to hear this word pop out of Davey's mouth, I mentally searched for a way to honor the moment and, voilà, moments of language became a new way to recognize my students' thinking. Later that day, during the afternoon read-aloud, Andres earned another moment of language for knowing that the idiom, "make a mountain out of a molehill" meant "don't make a big fuss" (see Figure 6.5).

❊　　　　　　❊　　　　　　❊

The following fall I prepare to welcome both kinds of moments. I do not have long to wait when, in mid-September, I close Byrd Baylor's *Everybody Needs a Rock* and ask, "What are you thinking about this story?"

"Was this fiction or nonfiction?" asks Olivia.

"Did this take place a long time ago or now?" Noah wonders.

I inwardly celebrate these excellent questions but decide to start off the year as I usually do, using moments of science to establish an environment of inquiry in my classroom. It is not until December that I introduce moments of language when my students begin noticing elements of writing craft in read-alouds and in their own independent reading books. Victoria recognizes a weather lead in *Poppleton in Spring* by Cynthia Rylant. Chase notices poetic language in *Raising Yoder's Barn* by Jane Yolen.

In April we are working on informational text, and Daniel wants to know whether you can write a nonfiction book about a fictional character. I tell Daniel that he has discovered (inadvertently) a new genre—literary criticism—and earned himself a moment of language. I introduce the idea of a movie or book review as a special kind of writing where an author might describe a character, and I make a note to bring in a *New York Times Book Review* section the following day.

One day I am surprised to find a moment of language popping up during a math discussion. We are talking about tables as a way to organize information for making a graph when Paige raises her hand to declare, "It's like a table of contents, which helps you organize information in a book."

"You are absolutely right, Paige. I have never made that connection before," is my spontaneous reply. As I record Paige's moment of language, I appreciate again how these moments keep me engaged in the learning process and my own sense of wonder.

Some moments of language may seem mundane, like the time Kaitlyn notices the color gray is spelled two different ways—with an *a* and an *e* in the same book about cats—and Daniel reports that his mother taught him this kind of mistake is called a typo. Other moments are nothing short of sublime. One day I sit down to start the next chapter in *Ereth's Birthday* by Avi when Samantha's hand flies urgently into the air.

"Laurie, I just realized that when I'm listening to a book like *Ereth's Birthday*, that doesn't have a lot of pictures, I'm visualizing." It is an amazing "aha" moment for Samantha, and the chills take a few trips up and down my back as I add her moment to our list.

Although I invent the term *moments of language*, it is my students who initiate and cultivate these moments as another comprehension strategy—the reading/writing connection. Their awareness of language in the form of writing craft, vocabulary, genre, and text structure not only enriches their reading comprehension but also sets them up to become proficient writers. I remember the many reading conferences I attended where teachers posed the same question to published children's book authors, over and over, "How can I help my students become better writers?" The answer, bar none, was always, "Read, read, read." In other words, by reading and absorbing literary language, young children will learn to read "like writers." In fact and over time, I recognize that my most poetic, descriptive writers, students who use dialogue effectively, who "show, don't tell," are often the most passionate readers.

From placing *metacognition* on a word list to witnessing an eight-year-old's sophisticated metacognitive process blossom before me, moments of language continue to raise the bar of critical thinking skills in my classroom.

CHAPTER 7

Literacy Through Nature Study— Writing

When I began my career as a first-grade teacher, daybooks were the established convention for teaching writing. While students dictated a sentence or two about a personal experience, teachers, parents, or paraprofessionals wrote their ideas in neat manuscript on widely spaced solid lines with a middle dotted line to guide the formation of lowercase letters. Then our first graders each drew a picture to accompany their stories and eventually might pen their own inventive spelling. That same year, however, the writing process was introduced in my district, and I soon learned to move my young authors through prewriting, drafting, revision, and publication. Whatever the format for telling personal stories, the common wisdom also advocated providing experiences for students to write about, and often class books were created around Our Trip to the Fire Station or Making Applesauce.

Years later I rediscover the good sense of offering shared adventures—but this time in the natural world. The combination of our stream visits; bird study;

and continuous presentation of rocks, feathers, bones, and creatures in the classroom maintains our focus on nature and the environment and gives my students a ready-made treasure chest of topics to write about. Nature journals are a place to record our experiences and observations as they happen, but they can also serve as writer's notebooks and scientific lab notebooks. During writing workshop our experience in the natural world inspires our writing in a variety of genres—personal narrative, poetry, and nonfiction (see Figure 7.1).

NATURE JOURNALS

We are just gathering on the rug after gym class when Christopher yells out, "Robin!"

"Are you sure, Christopher?"

"Yes, I'm sure," he insists.

Off to the windows we fly on this morning in mid-March to look for the most celebrated sign of spring in upstate New York, and, sure enough, three robins

FIGURE 7.1 - Writing workshop in my classroom. The windows look out on the small woods and our bird feeder.

are hopping along on the grass. As we watch, children offer their observations, first the obvious features—red breast and yellow beak—followed by behaviors (see "Writing Workshop—Personal Narrative" later in this chapter).

"When it walks, it's not like us. It takes lots of little fast steps."

"When it walks, it puts its head down."

"When it bends its head down, the tail spreads out."

"Laurie, I think we know what a robin looks like now."

This comment is from Peter. I know from his mom that he loves our bird study, but in class, he is measured about his contributions to our discussions.

"I agree, Peter. Do you think we should stop observing now?"

"No, let's keep looking out the window."

We watch long enough to see a robin tugging on something. My eyes are slow to focus, but a few students assure me it is a worm.

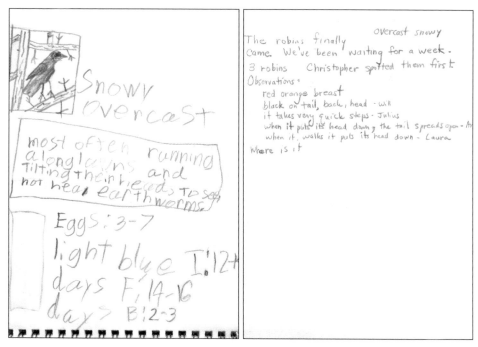

FIGURE 7.2 (LEFT) - Julius creates his own field guide page for the American robin.
FIGURE 7.3 (RIGHT)- Another typical journal entry for me. I manage to record some of my students' observations and then stop in midsentence, most likely diverted to help a student!

"I think this is a nature journal moment," I announce and in less than five minutes, you can hear a pin drop. By now my students are accustomed to such a swift change of plans when it comes to appreciating the natural world, and I have already made my peace with abandoning our routine this morning. I decide the read-aloud can wait until tomorrow. Some students grab field guides and start drawing. Julius starts copying robin facts from the Stokes field guide (see Figure 7.2). I teach Hannah how to use an index because her attempts to find the American robin using color tabs are unsuccessful. Will decides to record his new insight—"the robins can't find worms when there is a lot of snow on the ground so they come when the snow is gone." Christopher asks if he can earn a moment of science. He seems satisfied when I tell him that my nature journal will say Christopher was the one to spot the robin first (see Figure 7.3).

Twenty minutes later, as my students finish up their entries, our peaceful delight with the natural world floats around the room. I reach for Rachel's writing folder to read the poem she composed during writing workshop that very morning (see Figure 7.4).

Robin

Yank tug pull
Wiggle around,

You are a sign
of spring,

that is why
you tug
    tug
      tug
        tug
until you get
your worm.

FIGURE 7.4 - This poem literally flows out of Rachel's pencil as she experiments with line breaks.

Nature journaling is an integral part of the writing practice in my classroom. If a week should go by without using journals, someone in my class is sure to ask why. The groundwork for valuing nature journals begins during the first three days of school when I convey their importance in my own life. Throughout the month of September, all my students share Life Boxes, introduced after reading *Wilfred Gordon McDonald Partridge* by Mem Fox. (This is an idea I found in a long-forgotten teacher magazine and tweaked for my purposes.) Wilfred Gordon, a small boy, visits ninety-six-year-old Miss Nancy in a nursing home and helps her remember significant events in her life when he gives her a basket containing five of his most precious possessions.

In my first newsletter home, I explain the story of Wilfred Gordon and include the following assignment:

Please help your children identify five important people, places, or activities in their lives and collect objects or photos to represent them. We would like to display each life box for several days before it goes back home. We look forward to getting to know each other better!

I share my Life Box first to model how an object represents what is important to me. Out of a miniature wicker suitcase, I slowly remove my suede, rhinestone-covered ballroom shoes, a portable microphone, a garden trowel, a family photo, and my nature journal, explaining how each represents one of my loves: dancing, singing, gardening, family, and the natural world.

The day I share my nature journal, Sydney and Kaitlyn decide to make journals of their own during afternoon activity time. Over three days they use tree field guides to trace and copy pictures of trees and then add labels. Kaitlyn staples her homemade book; Sydney punches holes and binds hers together with string. As soon as they share their journals with the class, I announce that tomorrow everyone will decorate a personal nature journal to use in school (see Chapter 1, Tip #9).

To encourage my students to be attentive to the natural world at home and to instill the habit of keeping a nature journal on hand, I assign Nature Journaling at Home soon after our second stream study visit. Although most students will observe something outside, indoor houseplants or pets are included as possible subjects in case a family outing cannot be arranged. I include the assignment in my next newsletter.

Your children will be doing some nature journaling for homework. Please encourage them to include drawings and written observations or questions. Use one side only and stay within the black border because we will cut and paste this homework into our nature journals at school (see Figure 7.5).

The space for writing and drawing matches the size of our nature journal pages, which is where the homework will ultimately be saved. When all the home journal entries are returned, we share them within stream groups, then

FIGURE 7.5 - An example of a completed entry for Nature Journaling at Home.

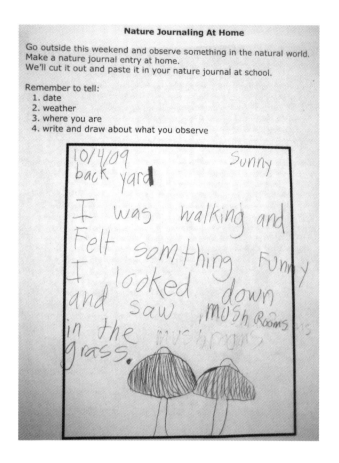

cut and paste them onto the next blank nature journal page (see Figure 7.6). In my group, Joey, proud of his experience, is eager to share.

I went to Camp Barton and found 26 newts. Why are there are so many? Why are the back legs longer than the front?

Then, with eyes twinkling, Joey tells us, "When I was 'observating' the newts, I didn't have my nature journal with me, so when I got home I looked them up and 'observated' on the computer." I remind him about the time I looked up water striders online and discovered that water striders had six legs, not four.

Every year a few students are inspired to continue nature journaling at home. One day in November, Luis brings in a plastic bag filled with five little home-

FIGURE 7.6 - Sydney draws a picture of her "secret place, a tree [whose] leaves are changing colors."

made nature journals, one for himself and extras for his friends. He shows the class how he cut 8½-by-11-inch white paper in half and stapled several sheets together. On the cover is a drawing of the hole he and his friends found on the playground, and each page has the headings "Date" and "Weather."

"I stayed up very late last night to work on it," he tells us proudly.

He pulls out a ruler and a thermometer, explaining that, "as we [he and his friends] dig, we can measure how deep the hole is and also see how cold it is."

Right after Thanksgiving vacation, Victoria hands me a note when she walks through the door.

Happy Thanksgiving Laurie. I hope you had a nice Thanksgiving. I did some stuff we do in stream study. I did depth with my dad. It was six inches and I did the speed. It was two seconds.

She shows me the record of her findings, an exact replica of our stream study chart:

Depth	*Dad and Victoria*	*6 inches*
Speed	*Mom and Victoria*	*2 seconds*

Nature journaling during stream study is just the beginning. There are six or seven weekly opportunities to journal at the stream before we shift to monthly visits in November and move our nature journaling indoors. While observing wildlife outside our classroom window my students strengthen their appreciation of the natural world and develop their journaling skills at the same time.

One morning I sit down next to the window with Shaundra to conference about one of her stories. Daniel, at a nearby table, softly pronounces "squirrel" and walks toward us. I turn in time to see a gray squirrel that has made its way past the baffle of our bird feeder, holding on to the pole right beneath the wooden feeding platform, ready to scramble to the platform itself. A few more students make their way to the windows, so I turn and announce to the rest of the class, "We have a little situation here. There's a squirrel about to get on the feeder." Everyone comes over and we watch (I have to admit, with delight) as the squirrel looks tentatively around, stretches out its body, and, in a flash, lands on the roof of the feeder, where it looks around again before jumping down to the feeding tray. We watch while the squirrel grasps seed after seed in its two front paws, nibbling away.

"Let's knock on the window and see if he'll jump off," I finally suggest, not quite resigned to the quantity of seed being consumed.

It takes ten knocks before the squirrel notices and jumps down but within seconds, it returns.

"This is a moment we do not want to forget," I whisper. "Pack up your writing folders, and I will pass out your nature journals."

There is something magical about capturing this collective experience immediately on a journal page. Very soon everyone is involved in writing, drawing, and adding color to their entries (see Figure 7.7). In the middle of her drawing, Shaundra points to the carpet of seeds on the ground beneath the feeder and wonders for the first time if they are whole or just empty shells.

"What do you think?" I ask everyone sitting nearby.

Shaundra imagines half and half. Olivia agrees. Helena thinks they are all empty and Wendy agrees with Helena.

When everyone is gathered on the rug sharing squirrel entries with a partner, we close our nature journaling session by discussing ideas about the birdseed. Ultimately we all agree with Luis.

"I think they must all be empty because if not the squirrels would have food on the ground and wouldn't have come up on the feeder."

Over and over again these kinds of discussions evolve from observation followed by nature journaling. When we slow down and take time to examine our world, my students reflect and instinctively practice the writer's adage, "Writing is thinking. To write well is to think clearly" (McCullough 2003). Again I

FIGURE 7.7 - Sydney labels the feeder parts: *top of the feeder, squirrel, seeds, suet, wood, baffle,* and *pole.*

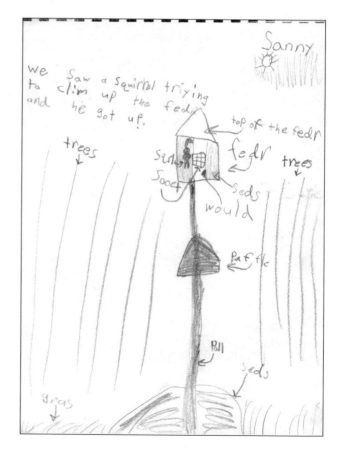

affirm for myself the importance of drawing since, in Shaundra's case, it is her drawing of the feeder and ground below that inspires her question.

If two weeks should go by without remarkable sightings in the great outdoors, I look for other ways to keep nature journaling a consistent part of our writing practice. Nature journals are a place to question, hypothesize, list, record, describe, narrate, reflect, express feelings, or compose a poem. They are also home to observational drawings, sketches, charts, and diagrams. In January, after observing birds at the feeder for two months, I ask my students to become experts on one particular bird and practice identifying important features at the same time.

"You know, artists and scientists have a lot in common. They both observe the world around them very carefully. If you draw a plant or an animal in the natural world, you will never forget it.

"I want you to choose a bird that you don't know very well or one that does not come very often. Then find an illustration or a photograph in one of our field guides and use it to make a detailed drawing in your nature journal. When you are finished, add color and label the most important features to help identify your bird."

"Should we put the name of the bird on the page?" asks Sydney.

"That's an excellent idea. If you know the name, that bird will be your friend forever."

Another day we take our nature journals to the computer lab and visit the All About Birds site, maintained by the Cornell Lab of Ornithology. Students choose between two new birds recently sighted at the feeder, the northern flicker and the chipping sparrow. As I circulate, admiring stunning detailed drawings, I recognize an opportunity to assess my students' reading and writing. My anecdotal records reveal a wide range of ability from Jocelyn and Nicholas, who complete the assignment supported by their special education teacher, to Victoria, who is capable of reading and synthesizing the text in her own words (see Figure 7.8).

In between is Chase, a skilled decoder and a major birder who copies information word for word and cannot tell me where to look for northern flickers because he mindlessly copies, "and you may be surprised that the birds can be found on the ground."

FIGURE 7.8 - Victoria records short notes about the northern flicker: "black bib on upper breast, round eye, breast tan with spots, lives in wood and near woods, usually feeds on ground."

In April and May our classroom is home to a variety of insects in all different stages of life cycles. The painted lady butterfly is a pupa; the silkworm moth is in the voracious larval stage, eating tablespoonfuls of mulberry leaf mash each day; the milkweed bug habitat is filled with nymphs. Every few days we use graphic organizers provided by the science kit company to record our weekly observations. One day, halfway through our insect study, I reach for our nature journals instead.

"I worry that these pieces of paper in your science folders will get lost one day, but I hope you will keep your nature journals for the rest of your lives," I say in a hushed voice.

Nineteen pairs of bright eyes look back at me. I can almost hear the wheels clicking as these seven- and eight-year-olds try to imagine "the rest of their lives." For me it is an obvious choice since our nature journals are the place we record information and reflections about the natural world. I truly do hope that my students will treasure and keep their journals, unlike the assortment of worksheets and loose papers that must surely end up in the recycle bin at the end of the school year.

I demonstrate how to draw a line dividing the journal page in half. The top will illustrate the entire habitat; the bottom will zoom in on an individual animal. For example, the silkworm page shows a patch of food covered with larvae on the top and a close-up view of one larva on the bottom. I pass out the journals, and as students are recording the date and weather, I deliver silkworms to each table.

Most students begin writing and drawing pretty quickly after a few minutes of observation. When they finish their silkworm observations, they move on to

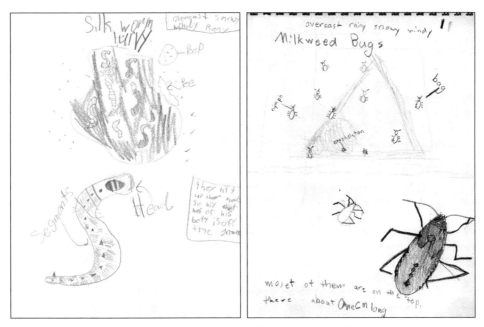

FIGURE 7.9 (LEFT) - Sydney nicknames her silkworm *lurvy*. She continues to enjoy using labels and notes: "they lift up their heads so high that half of his body is off the ground." **FIGURE 7.10 (RIGHT)** My students automatically record the weather even though we are observing inside the classroom. The milkweed bug habitat is on top, and a detailed close-up of one milkweed bug is on the bottom.

FIGURE 7.11 - Charlotte writes about the first birds that come to our feeder and adds a question: "why do we mostly see blue jays?"

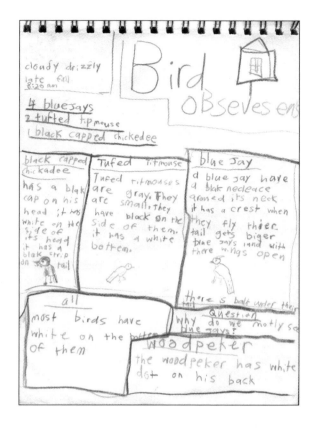

the milkweed habitats. As they work, I choose a few entries to highlight to the class for inspiration (see Figures 7.9 and 7.10). Labels are the finishing touch, thus preparing my students for the labeled diagrams they will include in their upcoming nonfiction books. I am pleased to see how independent my students have become; only one student needs support.

Our nature journals are an important writing tool throughout the year. For some students they serve as a writer's notebook, a collection of impressions, understandings, and experiences they can turn to when ready to start a new story. In addition to stream study, we use them for observations at the bird feeder (see Figure 7.11); on field trips to the nature center (see Figure 7.12) and to the Cornell Lab of Ornithology; when guests bring special presentations to our school like the live eagles and owls from Cornell University's Raptor Program; and to record the drawings, hypotheses, experiments, and observations that inform our other science explorations.

FIGURE 7.12 - My students happily translate their nature-journaling skills to new venues. In this entry Sophie records what she hears and sees as she walks the nature center trails.

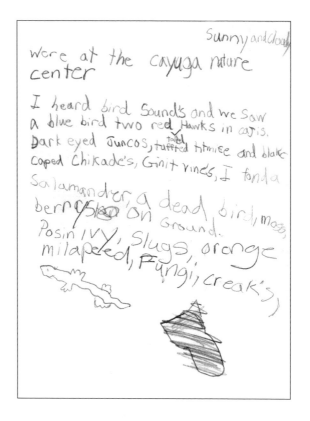

WRITING WORKSHOP: PERSONAL NARRATIVE

We are almost two weeks into the school year, and I worry that no animals have appeared outside our classroom window. How will I start training my students to observe the natural world? I am in the middle of scribbling myself a note to investigate my own backyard after school when Luis walks in with a caterpillar to share. We put this potential cousin to a woolly bear in the center of the rug, and I suggest we observe what it looks like and what it is doing. We note:

- Black and yellow near head
- Walks on many legs and uses them all at the same time
- Has hairs and some are longer than others

Luis, who picks up the caterpillar, explains that it can stick to things. "It poops" goes on the list when he shows the droppings in his hands.

The next day I write Features and Behaviors on the whiteboard and together we organize our information about Luis's caterpillar. Later I will transfer our list to a piece of chart paper to use as a reference for future observations.

Features:
- Brownish-orange hairs that look like fur
- Black head
- Yellow stripe on head
- Hairs of different lengths
- Long hairs are white and wispy

Behaviors:
- Poops black dome-shaped droppings
- Crawls around using all of its legs
- Lifts and wags its head
- Sticks to a surface upside down

I introduce some new vocabulary—*wispy*, *dome-shaped*, *droppings*—and in less than ten minutes, we have established a system for categorizing observations. Over time I realize that this exercise of naming features and behaviors prepares my second-grade writers to include rich details in their personal stories.

In fact, explorations in the natural world offer abundant material for my students' narrative writing. By the third week of school my students figure out that if they bring in a caterpillar, an unusual rock, or a giant leaf, they will be rewarded with profuse smiles and exclamations from their teacher. Sharing is a requirement in my classroom, so we wait until everyone takes a turn before starting the next round. Soon all manner of invertebrates, bones, rocks, wildflowers, and exoskeletons pour in steadily. The morning nature shares that follow serve as rehearsals for writing personal stories.

One morning Sabina brings in a container filled with water, rocks, and a three-quarter-inch-long crayfish she found in a creek. As she begins to explain how she found it, she instinctively narrates her discovery with a clear beginning, middle, and end. I suddenly recognize in her story the oral exercise my students repeat with their writing partners every day. I waste no time in making it a regular practice to connect these morning shares with potential stories to write.

Beginning—"Well I went to my recorder lesson and played in a creek there."

Middle—"I was picking up rocks, looking for things. First I tried to catch a newt, but then I found the crayfish and asked my mom if I could take it home."

End—"My mom said no but when I asked if I could take it to school, my mom said yes."

Sabina's crayfish is a big hit as she walks around the circle letting it crawl from one hand to the next.

"What a smart writer you are, Sabina," I point out, acting as if she had every intention of writing about her crayfish today. "Not only did you figure out the beginning, middle, and end of your crayfish story but you *zoomed* in the middle showing us how you picked up rocks until you found the crayfish."

The *zooming* connects to our use of hand lenses at the stream.

"Just like we use hand lenses to uncover details of the natural world," I remind everyone, "we need to include details in a story to make it come alive for our readers."

Another day Eric shares his snakeskin during morning meeting. He also tells a story, although it is very brief, that can serve as a writing rehearsal.

Beginning—"We were at a lake."

Middle—"We were looking around in the woods and we saw a spider web."

End—"The snakeskin was on the web."

This is a serendipitous moment for Eric, who is not a confident writer. When his classmates start asking questions—"Where was the lake?" "Who were you with?"—Eric is willing to concede that his snakeskin story might be worth recording on paper. I quickly segue into writing workshop with a lesson on how to write a 4W beginning, answering the questions who, what, when, and where.

I open the pad of chart paper to a story I wrote about finding starfish on Salt Spring Island. My demonstration stories are almost always about my own adventures in the natural world.

David and I walked down to the water on Salt Spring Island to see what we could find.

When I reread the beginning, my students are quick to help me revise the lead. "You didn't say *when,* Laurie!"

Last summer David and I walked down to the water on Salt Spring Island to see what we could find.

As I send my students off to their writing seats, I write "4W BEGINNINGS" in big letters on the whiteboard and invite them to sign up underneath the heading if they try one today. Six students, including Eric, sign up to share. This is a technique I use whenever I introduce a new piece of writing craft. The appeal of writing one's name with a special marker is apparently enough to motivate otherwise cautious writers to try something for the first time.

In November when we begin to work on revision, Shaundra, one of my struggling writers, chooses one of her very first stories about stream study. In the middle she writes, "We have fox-walked."

"Let's add some detail to that. How do you fox-walk?"

"You crouch down, tiptoe."

At my request, Shaundra crouches down next to her desk and demonstrates. "What else do we do?"

"Look all around."

I help her remember that we are also quiet, and then we move to her next sentence, "I found a salamander."

"What did it look like?"

"It was greenish-brownish, wiggly."

"What was wiggly?"

"The whole body. I put leaves in my hand and then the salamander crawled into my hand."

Our revision conference is successful because Shaundra remembers so many vivid details about her experience at the stream. I praise her for *showing, not telling*, jot down a few key words on a sticky note, and leave her to add more information on her own.

As other students finish revising old stories and start writing new ones, I notice that stream study and birds at the feeder are popular topics (see Appendix A). For example, when Jocelyn returns from a long absence, I am not surprised that she chooses to write about the bird feeder. She is the one who first identified the downy woodpecker by the white "spots" on its wings, and she is very proud of her reputation. Nature study is at the forefront of our minds all day long. No wonder my students are drawn to writing about the investigations that enthrall and engage them.

When I first started stream study I had no idea that our adventures in the natural world would become my most effective tools for teaching literacy skills back in the classroom. Now when I respond to the perennial question, "What should I write about?" I can tap into our collective experiences at the stream for prompts. Sabina also reminds me that my students cannot help but be influenced by my living and breathing passion for all living plants and animals. After a three-week unit on editing for proper word spacing, letter formation, punctuation, and spelling, my students choose one story to "fix up" and mail to someone as a gift. Motivation for a thorough job of editing is high since most of these second-grade authors will not be around to translate. Sabina, however, chooses to give her bird feeder story (see Figure 7.13) to me and attaches an accompanying note:

Dear Laurie,

I'm giving you a story that I wrote. I fixed up the periods and capitals and word wall words and spelling. I hope you will like it. It is about your bird feeder and birds. I know you like birds. That's why I'm giving it to you. Have fun reading it.

From, Sabina

FIGURE 7.13 - On this middle page of Sabina's story she notes the *behavior* she observed shortly after we filled the bird feeder with seed for the first time.

Name _____ Date NOV. 19

Sad in lee we saw three birds flying to the bird feader. and we saw a beahavyer. They never take the ferst seed they see. They look for the one they want and push off the ones they didint like.

POETRY

As we transition into writing poetry, the natural world continues to inspire my students as they write poem after poem about streams, seasons, weather, plants, and animals. After writing poetry for a month some of my students still need more experience in how to choose a topic and generate language expressive of their thoughts and feelings, so I decide it is time to write a class poem.

"We know that poets write about things that give them a *big feeling.* If we were going to write a poem about what gives us a big feeling as a class, what could we write about?" (Several ideas for teaching poetry are inspired by Lucy Calkins's [2003] *Units of Study for Primary Writing, Poetry: Powerful Thoughts in Tiny Packages.*)

The first two responses are flattering—"Laurie." "Laurie reading."—but I am hoping for more. When Jade says, "birds," a few hands go down.

"I'm going to add to Jade's idea—anything in the natural world," adds Samantha.

When Wendy says, "stream study," I jump in.

"Since there are three ideas from the natural world, let's choose one—how about watching birds together? What object or moment or detail can we use to hold our big feeling about birds?"

"The red-bellied woodpecker."

This suggestion comes from Wendy, who, though usually quiet, is very involved in our discussion. In fact, she has made a good choice, since the red-bellied's arrival at the feeder always inspires an impressive chorus of oohs and aahs. I take the red-bellied woodpecker photo off the window near the feeder and tape it to the easel chart in front of the room.

"Let's make of a list of words that we think of when we watch the red-bellied."

- Pecking at the tree
- Eating suet
- Has stripes
- Bright red head

When Jocelyn, who rarely raises her hand, says "big," I immediately validate her contribution before we continue brainstorming.

"You're right, Jocelyn. When the red-bellied arrives, it feels really big to us."

"A big red blob on its head."

Daniel yells out, "hat," and everyone breaks into a smile.

"Cap."

"True, but ornithologists *often* talk about the cap on a bird. How can we see it with poets' eyes?"

"Baseball cap with a visor or big red baseball cap?"

"It startles us when it comes to the feeder."

This last type of sentiment is often missing from many of my students' poems. They have learned to use words that describe the subject of their poems but not how to evoke a feeling or a connection. By working on a class poem, my hope is that together, we will begin to generate more ideas like Samantha's "it startles us," thus providing necessary models and giving my students more practice. At the same time, I celebrate the increased participation of normally reticent children in our poetry discussions. I am more and more convinced that their confidence and engagement is motivated by a connection to the natural world (see Appendix B).

NONFICTION

We spend the last two months of school writing nonfiction books. My students think about their expertise and make lists of potential topics they can teach. Choice is a powerful element in our writing workshop throughout the year, but since they will publish only one nonfiction book, I guide students in selecting their final subjects. I make sure they will be able to write for several weeks before doing additional research. (The format for teaching nonfiction writing is developed from Lucy Calkins's [2003] *Units of Study for Primary Writing: Reports and Procedures*.) Invariably each year, empowered to be experts on a species we have investigated together, six or seven students write books about the birds we watch outside or the trout and insects we examine in the classroom.

Daniel, for example, establishes his identity as a woodpecker expert in January when he brings in a two-foot section of a tree trunk cut from a tree in his yard. After he points out the woodpecker nest, visible through a perfectly round hole, Daniel proceeds to tell us everything he knows about downy woodpeckers, his best guess for which bird had made the nest. In April, when I report seeing a red-bellied woodpecker flying from our feeder to the same spot on the red oak behind it, I turn to Daniel, who immediately anticipates we will find a nest. We agree to check out the red oak on the way to the stream later that afternoon.

It was easy to predict that Daniel would choose to write a book about wood-peckers, and soon Chase and Eric join him. Chase and Daniel concentrate solely on woodpeckers, writing chapters on Food, Habitat, Different Kinds, Tips on Identification, Nests, How They Climb, and, of course, the rare or extinct ivory-billed. Eric includes woodpeckers as one chapter among others on birds of prey, waterbirds, and songbirds. As they begin to write, very different levels of proficiency emerge. Daniel borrows woodpecker books from the school library every week, devours them at home, proves to be an independent nonfiction writer, and produces his best writing of the year. Chase, a strong decoder, pores over field guides, but his sketchy comprehension results in erroneous facts popping up in every chapter. Eric produces a few sentences a day and sticks to very basic information. For example, he devotes a week to a chapter on bird-watching tools—a nature journal, binoculars, and colored pencils. Nevertheless the three become known as our experts whenever a woodpecker question emerges.

By mid-May Daniel is starting his ninth chapter and Eric is learning how to organize a chapter with an introductory sentence followed by supporting facts. Daniel confirms his understanding of zygodactyl feet (pairs of toes, two facing forward and two backward) (see Figure 7.14) while Eric uses our chart of important and interesting bird facts to choose and learn new facts independently such as, "small owls eat moths and insects." Each child in his own way learns more about the natural world within the context of writing nonfiction books.

In the meantime other students are close to finishing, so after school one day, I sit down to read all the drafts. That is when I discover Chase's creative text about woodpeckers' being endangered because sparrows are taking over their nests, and yellow-shafted flickers having yellow bellies. I meet with the three bird experts the following morning, and together we help Chase understand

FIGURE 7.14 - Daniel writes an entire chapter about zygodactyl feet.

that it is usually loss of habitat that endangers birds and that yellow-shafted refers only to the yellow beneath the wings. Part of my mini-lesson that day emphasizes the importance of making sure your facts are absolutely accurate when writing a "teaching text."

Right before Memorial Day weekend, I invite all parents and caregivers to a publication celebration. It is a time for each student to share a self-published nonfiction book with a parent, grandparent, or sibling, followed by lunch in the classroom. I work hard to ensure that every single student will be able to share with a family member, and, in some cases, I arrange for rides to school. As a last resort, I ask a student to name teachers they might like to invite and then find one whose schedule allows her to come, listen, and honor that student's work.

When everyone arrives, I explain our writing process and review the chart of nonfiction features we have studied together: an "all-about" title; a table of contents; an introduction (see Figure 7.15); sections or chapters; diagrams (see Figure 7.16); captions, words, or phrases in bold letters; "different kinds of" pages; interesting facts pages; how-to pages; and an index.

"Just as we observe the features and behaviors of insects and birds, we started our study of the nonfiction genre by examining the features of over forty nonfic-

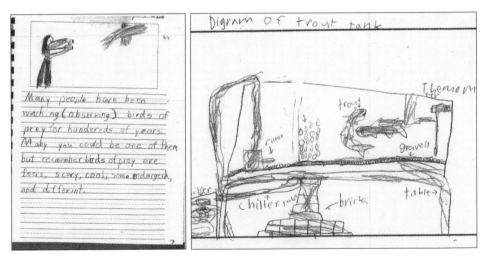

FIGURE 7.15 (LEFT) - Rachel's introduction to her book about birds of prey. **FIGURE 7.16 (RIGHT) -** Luke's trout tank diagram from his book entitled "The Trout Stuff."

tion books," I explain and, once again, affirm for myself the connection between our natural and literary worlds.

❋   ❋   ❋

At the end of the school year, after three months of writing poetry and nonfiction, we return to personal narrative in preparation for a final writing assessment. We review the elements of a good story, and I read a new one of my own about meeting a muskrat in a cornfield. When I send my students off to their seats, only one writer needs support choosing a topic. Within a few minutes everyone else is sketching and planning out stories. As I circulate around the room, I notice that almost half of the class has chosen to write about experiences in the natural world. Joey usually writes about finding snakes or frogs so that is no surprise, but Ben finds salamanders on a play date with Joey. Aurora writes about the first time a hummingbird came to our feeder. Rachel remembers watching a bird make a nest. Luke releases our trout. Shannon tries to catch tadpoles. Kevin discovers a Baltimore oriole in his backyard. Margot writes about the potato bug she just shared with the class. And Andres immortalizes his moth! (See Appendix A.)

The natural world is a steady source of inspiration for my second-grade writers throughout the year. From the first moments of nature journaling at the stream and the initial stories in September, to poetry, nonfiction text, and the more skillfully crafted narratives written in May, the natural world supports my students' development as successful writers *and* readers.

Our exploration in the natural world also levels the playing field for speaking and listening skills. Over time I have watched language-impaired students like Jocelyn join the conversation, spontaneously or with a timely nudge, eager to share their observations, discoveries, and, sometimes, even opinions.

Nature study provides a context and a reference point for a well-rounded language arts program. The natural world is a gift I welcome into my classroom every year, a gift that helps me guide my students toward healthy, flourishing, literary lives.

CHAPTER 8

Creating Stewards of the Natural World

It is the last stream study visit of the year. We have just spent half an hour writing final reflections in our nature journals—what we liked, what we learned, what we remember. There are lists, poems, narratives, and drawings. It is June, the day is warm and sunny, and today we plan to enjoy our stream, explore, and say good-bye—no measurements, no formal observations.

My group is the last to head upstream, but before we get to our sit spot, Danny and his entire group are at my side, a mix of excitement and concern written on their faces.

"Laurie, we have pollution!" Danny reports.

I always try to take my students' concerns seriously, but I assume he is referring to the foamy white bubbles that often accumulate in the rocks after the stream tumbles over a mini-waterfall. I am about to proclaim as much when Charlie points out the paint-spattered rocks, and I realize that these bubbles are whiter and oilier than usual. By now the whole class has arrived, and we spread out to look for more clues. Sure enough, not far away, we find white-paint-covered cloths thrown under some bushes. We are stunned and outraged.

Who would do this to our stream? we wonder. However, my students do not linger on this question because their stream has been violated and they want to clean it up, right now.

Back at the classroom we gather a stack of containers, spoons, ladles, anything we can find to skim paint from the water's surface. We return to the stream where everyone is energized and sets to work with purpose and determination. Some scrub paint off the rocks with old toothbrushes while others fill up a bucket with oily, murky water. I leave parents in charge and take a few scouts to explore the surrounding area where we find more bushes with seemingly spray-painted leaves. As we continue to work, we revisit our speculation about the culprits. Kids in the after-school program? Teenagers? Then the conversation turns to the importance of protecting our environment and animal habitats.

After school, when I take our principal, Patrick, out to the stream to present the evidence, I express the profound impact of this incident on my students. Patrick promises to call the village police and the next day Officer Bill solves the mystery. Right across the stream, in full view, he finds a team of house painters in the midst of applying another fresh coat of white paint to a private home. Apparently they decided to use our stream for a fast cleanup.

My students are not convinced that the subsequent punishment—a more thorough cleanup and a reprimand to never let it happen again—is fair or adequate. As their teacher, I struggle to explain why adults would pollute a stream. Who wants to be the one to tell eight-year-old children that there are people who make bad choices in the world? I waste no time in impressing on them that plants and animals need strong advocates, concerned citizens like themselves to preserve our wild, green spaces for generations to come.

The paint episode resonates with me all summer long. I wonder where my students will go from here. How will the experience of bonding with a stream, only to see it defiled, influence their future pursuits? I realize that no book, no video, no theoretical discussion could have as much potential for turning this group of second graders into future stewards of the natural world.

THE NATURAL WORLD INDOORS: EXPLORATION AND CHOICE

One way I can assess the impact of our nature-based curriculum is during Activity Time, a half-hour slot three times a week during which every student in my class may choose an activity—building in the block corner; working with paint, glue, or recycled materials in the art area; games; puppet shows; observing a cluster of mealworms; drawing; or simply curling up with a good book. (One at a time, during the first weeks of school, different areas of the room are opened up after a discussion on appropriate behavior and use of materials.) Since this is neither a time to finish incomplete work nor a reward for finishing work early, all my students, both skilled and struggling learners, participate and are free to move from one area to another.

Thus Activity Time facilitates a heterogeneous mix of children and values a broad range of intelligences. For example, a child who labors over simple text during independent reading but designs unique block structures may become the preferred building partner for more advanced readers. The mix of animal-loving students gathered together to observe mealworms might cut across more conventional groupings—social, economic, or skill based. Children are affirmed for a striking color choice in a painting, a symmetrical pattern block design, a knack for taking apart an old hair dryer, performing a song and dance routine, or welcoming a diverse group of students to join in a game of "school."

Activity Time is when children explore their interests, learn how to make a choice, work out their understanding of the world, and extend the concepts we study together. At any moment, as children try out different materials, they could also be engaged in language, reading, writing, science, art, social studies, and math. As I move around the room, I question, suggest, wonder, praise, and sometimes join in. I also find fresh ways to connect with my students, affirm new talents, and evaluate the pulse of the classroom as a community and a learning environment. When I add nature study to the second-grade curriculum, I begin to notice that creative extensions to our investigation, and appreciation and concern for the natural world, make an appearance during Activity Time.

For a while we have a run on bird feeders in the art area—tube, platform, and house varieties. There are bird nests, insect habitats, nature books, animal collages, and cardboard egg cartons filled with bottle-cap baby birds. One day Christopher takes four little plastic pudding cups and tapes them together end to end. He attaches a string to the cups, puts the string around his neck, and proudly wears his homemade binoculars on the bus ride home.

Periodically, in an effort to encourage everyone to try all areas of the room, I will assign a particular project. During the month of March, I ask every student to paint a bird on 18-by-24-inch construction paper to display in our classroom art gallery. This year there is a penchant for red-bellied woodpeckers. Helena paints a fat one, explaining that it is puffed up to keep warm for winter. Blue jays, cardinals, robins, hummingbirds, and goldfinches are other perennial favorites (see Figure 8.1). Many students also spend hours drawing birds or poring over field guides. One afternoon, Christopher and his friend Peter come across the red-breasted nuthatch in *Stokes Beginner's Guide to Birds*.

"Look, Laurie, it's the same as the white-breasted except it has red on it!"

"Why don't you get another field guide and find a picture of the white-breasted nuthatch. That red on the breast is actually very hard to see outdoors. Maybe you can compare the two and look for other more obvious differences."

It does not take long for them to find the striped head on the red-breasted before they go off to build with geoblocks.

FIGURE 8.1 - A student pays close attention to detail in this painting of a male American goldfinch.

The day in May I put up the hummingbird feeder, two new birds appear. The chipping sparrow comes during math so we take a quick break, go to the windows, and share our observations: rusty head, black eye stripe, and white belly. As we are about to pull ourselves away, the hummingbird arrives and an excited chorus of voices fills the room—"I've never seen a hummingbird before!"

When Activity Time begins, I remind my class that bird identification is a possible choice. Shannon, Rachel, Laura, and Margot grab field guides and in a very short time find the chipping sparrow. All of a sudden Shannon spots yet another new bird at a distance, foraging on the grass. Ben and Will join in as everyone grabs binoculars. It is challenging to notice the details, and I keep asking, "What else do you see?"

It has a red head.

It's eating worms because its head is going up and down.

It looks like a kind of woodpecker.

Finally the bird turns around so everyone sees the black crescent. Field guides fly open to brightly colored photos of the northern flicker. I read aloud, "Flickers are often found on the ground, eating ants, their favorite food." I point out that *our* flickers are on a dry patch of soil, a possible anthill. Taking in the big smiles, animated voices, and bodies fairly jumping up and down, I glance at the clock and realize that these students have transformed Activity Time into a birding expedition.

You might not imagine the contours and shapes of a forest or hillside showing up in the block corner, but a group of five girls works on building Sapsucker Woods and the adjacent Lab of Ornithology over the course of a week. They use small cylinders to make trees, wooden arches to place a pedestrian bridge over a meandering construction-paper blue stream and square, colored tiles to represent birds. They construct a parking lot, the main visitor's center, and a place to buy binoculars, and they hang a hand-lettered sign: Sapsucker Forest, No Hunting, Thank You.

Another time Luis organizes his friends Eric and Jade to build a factory that cleans water. When the trio share their structure with the class, each builder describes a different piece of the factory. Jade points out the machine that sucks up dirt (pieces of torn paper) from the water. Eric elaborates on an apparatus that extracts ocean water, adds clean water, and shakes it around so that you can no longer taste the ocean. Luis explains that the machine can only hold a certain amount of water at one time, so if there is a storm, it will start to break down.

"If a big wave comes, this tube will bend down so the water can't get in. And if there's lightning, there are dryers to dry off the tracks."

"You've thought of everything," I say with true admiration.

At the end of the school year, two months into the Deepwater Horizon disaster, I take Luis aside and confide, "I'm thinking about your machine to clean water. They need you in the Gulf of Mexico right now to help clean up that oil spill!"

ROLE MODELS FOR ENVIRONMENTAL ACTIVISM

As nature study becomes an integral part of my second-grade curriculum and with students like Luis in mind, I also begin searching for ways to increase my students' environmental awareness and to provide models of real people working to preserve our natural heritage. In December, when I gather biographies from our school library for an annual study of peacemakers, I look for stories and picture books, accessible to second graders, about conservationists and environmental activists. Soon one of our favorite read-alouds is the story *Rachel Carson* by William Accorsi. My students often refer back to her love of nature and how she helped protect the birds from DDT exposure.

Throughout the year, we continue to read stories that emphasize the importance of protecting the natural world. *She's Wearing a Dead Bird on Her Head* by Kathryn Lasky and David Catrow is based on the true story of Harriet Hemmenway and her cousin Minna Hall, who decide to take on the late-nineteenth-century fashion of using feathers, wings, and whole bird bodies to adorn ladies' hats. In 1896 they establish the Massachusetts Audubon Society and use the group's political power to have a Massachusetts law passed outlawing trade in wild bird feathers.

One year Eva asks, "Laurie are there any peacemakers alive making the world a better place *today*?" An "aha" moment for me as a teacher, Eva's question makes me recognize, for the first time, that the preponderance of peacemakers we study are long departed. That night I am busy researching contemporary activists whose stories are easily translated to second graders. I find a video clip of Wangari Maathai, the founder of the Green Belt Movement in Kenya, who tells a Japanese folktale about a hummingbird trying to put out a forest fire one drop of water at a time. When the other larger and stronger animals like the elephant question her usefulness, the hummingbird, and Maathai, make the point that when you are feeling overwhelmed and powerless, when it feels like a problem is too big, everyone needs to do the best they can, and that, collectively, we can make a difference. In Maathai's case, she made a difference by starting a movement to reforest her native land, planting one tree at a time.

Another more modern environmental success story is that of Marion Stoddart, who organized her neighbors and the wider community in the mid-1960s to clean up the polluted Nashua River running through Massachusetts and New Hampshire. Lynne Cherry chronicles this tale in *A River Ran Wild*. Marion and her allies, through petition drives and grassroots organizing, eventually stopped the paper mills from dumping chemicals and dyes into the river and helped pass the first statewide clean water act in the nation.

Flute's Journey, a fictional tale by Lynne Cherry, weaves an environmental story focused on habitat loss and how it impacts the migration path of the wood thrush. Cherry describes the fundraising efforts started by children to plant more trees and save the Monteverde Cloud Forest Preserve in Costa Rica.

These stories set the stage for my class to take on a project of our own. Sometime in May, my students decide to raise money for one or more organizations supporting animals and habitat preservation. Over time favorite choices are the Rainforest Alliance, the World Wildlife Fund, and, closer to home, the SPCA. We have helped plant trees and build bridges for Mono Titi monkeys in the rain forest, adopted a manatee, and purchased pet supplies. I arrange for a local business to donate the cost of cards and printing, and soon my students embrace a plan to design and sell animal cards—simple line drawings on the front, simple animal facts they research on the back. As well as providing a satisfying end-of-year activity, I am also hoping to promote their future activism.

INQUIRY OVER TIME

Richard Louv wonders who will be the future stewards of our natural world when he makes the case for a "nature-child reunion" in *Last Child in the Woods: Saving Our Children from Nature-Deficit Disorder*. Published in 2005, his book began a conversation that spread across our nation in state and national legislatures, conservation groups, schools and businesses, government agencies, and civic organizations. He pointed out how environmental science was all but disappearing from our schools as they struggled to meet the demands of high-stakes testing in language arts and mathematics.

I realize it is entirely possible that my students may not encounter another nature-based program in their public school career unless they elect to take an environmental science class in high school. So I often wonder how much of our second-grade nature study will stay with them over time.

Our upstate New York landscape is covered with fossil-filled shale rock. My students are just as likely to uncover fossils on the playground during recess as along our rocky streambed. Early in the year, Peter shares a piece of shale split into three perfectly smooth horizontal slabs. Motivated by his fascination, I decide to ask Dr. Evans, a retired professor, to visit our classroom with his rock collection. Peter, who keeps his split rock wrapped carefully in a paper towel, remembers to bring it back to school and asks Dr. Evans to explain about the cracks. Peter is pleased to have his rock valued and center stage. Months later, he continues asking questions in his nature journal. Next to a drawing of a big rock, he asks, "Why is there a hole?" Next to a drawing of an oddly shaped rock, he asks, "Why is it that shape?" (see Figure 8.2).

During a spring field trip to release our trout fry, my students are spread along the stream bank drawing in their nature journals. Peter, attracted to a boulder on the opposite shore, is still puzzling over rock formations as he details the cracks and crevices in his journal. Finally, on our last walk up and down the streambed in June, when he points out other interesting rocks, I tell him that my brother is a geophysicist, and when he was in college, he learned all about rocks. I add that in high school Peter will be able to study Earth Science. "Yeah," he says nodding his head thoughtfully. "My sister took that."

For Shannon it is the ability to fly and defy gravity that intrigues her. In October she earns a moment of science for wondering how birds can fly if they are solid. I encourage her to go home and do some research and the very next day she breathlessly informs me that birds have hollow bones. Later in the year Shannon wonders why gravity does not make us fall backward when we are walking up hill. I immediately reference her earlier question about flying and then we talk about leaning forward when we walk up the steep gorges in our state parks. I do not worry about responding to Shannon with the precise physics of gravity but instead value the conversation as we try to figure it out by ourselves first.

FIGURE 8.2 - Peter's journal entries throughout the year reveal his fascination with rocks.

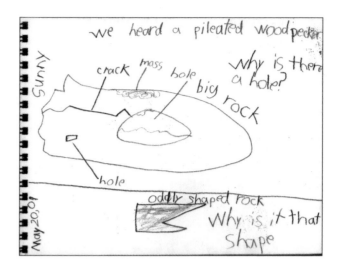

Noah establishes himself as our resident water expert. It starts at the stream, after the first heavy autumn rains, when he explains how air gets trapped to form bubbles in the water rushing over the rocks. During a series of water experiments, he quickly grasps how air pressure keeps a piece of paper toweling dry when it is stuffed into a vial and the open end is pushed underwater. Then one winter day he walks into the classroom and announces,

"Laurie, I had a moment of science at home. I wondered why only liquids freeze."

"How did that question come up for you, Noah?"

"I was in my car and I was thirsty and when I picked up my water bottle to get a drink, the water was all icy inside."

Daniel's passion for birds begins when the first scoop of black oil sunflower seeds fills our feeder. He remains on the rug one day in late November after I dismiss the class to their activity time choices.

"Laurie, why are some birds going extinct?"

"What do you think, Daniel?"

"People are killing them?"

I realize that Daniel is worrying about the red-headed woodpecker. A few weeks earlier, when my students were calling the red-bellied woodpecker red-*headed*, I pointed out that the red-bellied's name comes from the very small amount of red on its breast. When I continued to explain that there *is* another bird called the red-*headed* woodpecker, but that it is rare in New York, Daniel wanted to know why. Now, instead of answering Daniel, I ask him to think about why some birds might become rarer and promise to bring the question to the whole class. After lunch my students introduce the issues of climate change and loss of habitat.

Several months later, in mid-February, Daniel returns from a family vacation, sits next to me during our morning circle, and talks nonstop about the birds in Texas. He ignores my cues as I try, unsuccessfully, to start the day. "I saw the red-bellied, I saw the pileated. I saw the red-*headed* woodpecker, and, Laurie, it's not rare like we thought. It's just rare in New York, but I saw it in *Texas*." Daniel, the self-proclaimed advocate of red-headed woodpeckers, is jubilant.

These are the students I nurture throughout the year, hoping to keep them invested in the well-being of the natural world. I point out the connections they make as they return to a particular phenomenon over time. I value their developing expertise in a specific discipline and support their position as fellow teachers in our classroom learning community. Finally I encourage their ongoing inquiry and research as I emphasize their important role as future caretakers of planet Earth (see Figure 8.3).

STORIES AND GIFTS FROM THE NATURAL WORLD

When my students graduate to third, fourth, and fifth grade, they move down the hall and finally upstairs to an entirely different universe. Although my former students have always stopped by for a few months after second grade to say hello, I am delighted to find that after nature study, many, during their last three years in elementary school, continue to visit, stay in touch, and deepen our connection. They come to ask questions, share stories, or bring gifts from the natural world.

Ariella leaves a tree seed on my desk with an accompanying note, "I found this," and the very next day returns to ask if I know what it is. Andres is hanging up his coat in the hallway as I pass by.

"Laurie, I was looking at my nature journal last night."

"What were you looking at, Andres?"

"A downy woodpecker."

Knowing that Andres is a talented artist, I ask if he was admiring his drawing.

"Yes," he responds with a shy smile.

Before I return to my classroom, I urge him to show me his next entry.

FiGURE 8.3 - Theo identifies himself as a caretaker of the earth in his final journal entry of the year.

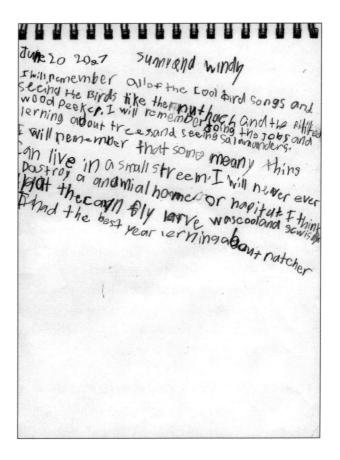

It is common for Ariella, Andres, and other third graders, whose classrooms are adjacent to mine, to stop by for a visit in the morning or after recess. When my former students in fourth and fifth grade, whose paths I rarely cross, begin to seek me out, I pay attention. Ana finds me after school as I walk back up the steps from saying good-bye to my bus-riding students.

"Laurie, I saw some tracks in the snow outside my house, and I think they were like dog tracks because I could see the fingernails in the snow and I know that dogs walk with their fingernails out and cats don't. Remember when we learned about that in second grade? So I think it was probably a fox."

"You made a great inference, Ana," I say, fascinated that she has not forgotten the mystery of the cat and dog tracks in *How to Be a Nature Detective* by Millicent Selsam. As she looks up at me, bright-eyed, I am pleased to be the one person in school who she thought would be interested in her story.

The next day Ana is waiting for me again in front of the school.

"Laurie, do you remember what I made for you in second grade? Those little birds made out of bottle caps?"

And a month later Ana comes plowing through the deep snow in her sneakers to tell me about the bird feeders at her house.

"It's amazing, Laurie. Only chickadees and titmice come to the feeder near our kitchen window, but all the other birds go to the feeder on the porch."

"Ana, why do you think that's happening?" I ask.

"I think most birds don't like to get too close to people," she answers immediately, having obviously thought about this phenomenon.

Miryam surreptitiously drops off a single ginkgo leaf on my desk early in September. Each week I find a fresh leaf, but I only uncover my benefactor when the leaves have turned from green to yellow, and I catch a glimpse of her mom delivering a leaf in her stead. The following year, as a fifth grader, Miryam sends an e-mail:

> *This evening I went bicycling; later we bicycled into the school parking lot. When I was doing turns and twists and figure eights, the wind on my wrists felt like birds, lightly perching, and that reminded me of you. I felt like I was merging with the wind, the feeling is still with me, you know . . . in my heart I'm still twisting and turning, swooping through the light of the street lamps. I could go on but it's time for bed. Expect a ginkgo leaf tomorrow.*

After my recent retirement, e-mails became a more common form of contact. Sydney sends me one-liners and photographs:

> *I saw birds getting married; A sign of spring! I saw a bird building a nest; I saw this at an office. It is a huge sticker.* (Accompanied by a photo of songbirds in a bush) *Look what my grandma saw!* (Accompanied by a photo of a male pileated woodpecker.)

Samantha composes a small narrative, incorporating the writing craft—"show, don't tell" and "dialogue"—we worked on together in second grade.

Dear Laurie,

In the Adirondacks I got to enjoy birds too. I saw bald eagles, herons, king fishers, loons, ravens, and hawks. I also went fishing and caught a pike, pumpkinseed sunfish, and perch. I learned to kayak, row, and canoe.

We saw a bald eagle catch a fish and eat it on a big rock. The picture of the fish carcass below is of the leftover pieces of that fish. On the same day, when I got home I caught the pike!

I jumped up and down and yelled, "I caught a pike!!!" It had sharp teeth, a long tail, big fins and I could even see the holes for its ears. It was about a foot long and was the biggest fish I ever caught. I was very excited and for the next five minutes I needed a break!

I miss second grade with you and I hope you see rare birds soon.

Love,

Samantha

And Daniel, ever the teacher, ever the birdwatcher, writes:

Hi Laurie,

Hope you enjoyed your trip. Here is a picture I drew of a male bluebird feeding his nestling that I saw last year. The female bluebird is much duller than the male.

Love,

Daniel

In fact, Daniel's mom tells me early on that she and her husband, both avid birders, tried, with no success, to interest their children in bird-watching. She is very grateful for the focus on birds and other natural phenomena in school that have translated into family nature outings enjoyed by all.

Many parents report on their children's ongoing relationship with the natural world. Janet, the parent of a current fifth-grade student, stops by to tell me that a pileated woodpecker landed in her backyard. Her daughter, Sophia, yelled, "I have to get my nature journal," ran upstairs to get it, sat down at the kitchen table, and started to draw. Janet was amazed that she still had the journal and knew exactly where to find it.

In all my years of teaching, I have never received as much parental feedback about any other unit of study or learning experience as I have with nature study. Often I witness how my students' interest and enthusiasm have rubbed off on their parents. Miryam's mom shows up one day with the fruit of the goldenrain tree, a green Chinese lantern–shaped seedpod, wondering if I know it. When I attend the preschool graduation of my friend's son, followed by a potluck dinner for families outside under the trees, the father of a former student suddenly yells out, "Laurie, is that a downy woodpecker?" His identification is accurate, and I realize his daughter's interest in birding has become a family affair.

Other parents communicate electronically. Olivia's mom writes:

Her appreciation of nature is very strong and keeps growing. She finds all sorts of things outside and loves all the little creatures around our house, even the bugs. She has learned to mimic all the birdcalls (the ones in our yard, that is), and sometimes I think she actually communicates with them. Anyway, you gave her a wonderful year.

When Noah and his family move to Pennsylvania, his mom sends this e-mail:

Laurie, Noah, and Peter were talking about you all this morning on our visit to the national aviary!

Cherie writes the following while vacationing in Maine one summer:

Last night we decided to "be Laurie" since we were awakened by a loud, repeated hooting and screeching. We looked outside and got our field guide, which we learned how to use in second grade: we had a two-foot-

*tall barred owl in our tree. Then we went out in our PJs to make sure we
got a sketch into our nature journals.*

And at the end of the school year she writes:

*There have been so many incredible moments even in the short time I
have been around your room, things that I will remember forever. You
are having such a profound effect on the little scientists, the little artists, the little singers, the little naturalists, the little citizens of con-
science, an effect that cannot be adequately measured or understood by
the children or the parents for many years.*

FUTURE STEWARDS OF THE NATURAL WORLD

By mid-June we usually turn our total attention toward putting closure on our
year in second grade together. To that end, every year, my students work on a
Second Grade Memory Book. By reviewing their memories I can identify the
most engaging activities, projects, and learning experiences of the year and
evaluate their growth in writing at the same time. The last pages are for digital
photos selected from our Class History Book. In the past, before I included
nature study, most students chose pictures of friends or sometimes a photo of
a block or Lego structure. Ever since our class historians started taking photos
of the stream and every possible animal, plant, and rock discovered there, half
of the photos chosen connect to the natural world.

My students choose images of woodchucks, turkeys, squirrels, or birds
observed at the classroom window; salamanders found at the stream; rushing water; waterfalls; our classroom trout; the painted lady butterfly released
in spring; or a group of students examining mealworms. I am intrigued that
they choose more animal pictures than photos of themselves or their friends.
For me it is testimony that for my students, as for myself, nature study is the
indisputable central theme of our year together in second grade.

❄   ❄   ❄

One morning as I scurry around preparing for our end-of-year writing assessment, Paige arrives and hands me a plastic container. I am startled to find a live baby bird inside, a few feathers sticking out along its back like a Mohawk, and tossed beside it a half dozen black-oil sunflower seeds for food. I run over to the computer and quickly type in "Lab of Ornithology." I search the menu, but the bell is about to ring, students are arriving en masse, and in desperation, I type, "finding a baby bird." I quickly follow the link to a website where I read: "put the bird in a cardboard box with breathing holes; add something to keep it warm; don't feed it milk or honey; call a wildlife rehabilitator as soon as possible."

I call Debbie in the office, ask her to call the Lab of Ornithology for me and, while waiting for the answer, I find a shoe box, punch some holes in the top, put paper towels along the bottom, and give Paige a jug to collect warm water from the cafeteria. When she returns I put the warm water in a ziplock bag and lay the little guy down on the bag. He keeps rolling off and I keep propping him back up. The word soon comes over the loudspeaker that the best solution would be to put the bird back where it was found. In the meantime, we open the lid every half hour to check on our waif.

By the end of the day, our baby bird has many more feathers, lifts its head, and opens its beak. Paige is pretty sure there was no nest in sight, but she agrees to take home the baby bird and return it to her backyard. Back in the classroom I review the surprising events of the day and remember how Paige described her discovery.

Well last night I went out into the natural world looking for something. I saw something on the ground but I didn't realize it was a bird because it didn't look like a bird. Then I thought it was a dead bird so I scooped it up and put it in a container and that's when I saw that it was alive.

I linger on the words *I went out into the natural world looking for something,* release the hectic pace of the day, and feel immersed in a quiet wonderment. This is the connection I have been nurturing all year long, isn't it? The hope that my students will see the natural world as a place to visit and explore or to simply be, a place filled with beauty and surprise, adventure and peace. If my students feel a sense of belonging, cultivate a bond with the natural landscape of living plants and animals, won't they grow up to protect and defend it?

I believe that introducing our young children to the natural world as part of their public school education is our best insurance for creating stewards to protect the future health of our planet. Certainly there are other venues for connection to nature—scouting programs, family farms, gardens or camping trips, a grandparent, neighbor, or other intimate adult—but these will not be available to every child. How powerful then for students in rural, urban, or suburban communities to meet that intimate adult in the form of a teacher with a passion for plants, animals, and their habitats who will take a walk around the school, find a sit spot, smell the bark of a tree, notice the changing color of the sky, listen to the rustle of a squirrel digging for food, and decide to make nature study the heart of the curriculum.

Postscript

n retirement I luxuriate in waking up to my own natural rhythms, lingering over my morning tea and crossword puzzle, and finally planting an early vegetable garden. Although I try to take frequent walks in the exquisite Ithaca gorges, along Cayuga Lake, and through our country woods, I begin to miss the interaction with children in the natural world. I decide to offer an after-school enrichment class for third through fifth graders, hoping that my former students will sign up. I am also curious to see how older students will navigate the stream site and whether their nature journal entries will be more detailed or evocative.

I call my class Making Friends in the Natural World and invite children to "come explore the woods behind our school and meet the plants and animals that live there." Most who enroll are indeed my former students. Some attend multiple times and others just once. The fourth time I offer the class, siblings of former students begin to appear. At first I am disappointed that my class does not attract more newcomers, but I soon come to appreciate the power of a teacher's passion conveyed in her subject matter, the connection to her students, and a shared sense of place. In the end it makes total sense that my students would be especially drawn to an experience that is so familiar and positive.

I start each session asking, "Why did you sign up for nature study?" My own students usually want to return to the stream they remember so well. Others mention their love of nature or animals or simply say, "I like being outside."

When we reach the stream site I smile with quiet appreciation as my students return to their past sit spots, point out the place where Samantha noticed evidence of deer sleeping in the snow, or make comparisons to their second-grade experience in their journals: "water deepish, not as much as *our* stream!" One fourth grader writes, "When I went outside for the first time in the school woods, I felt like I had come home from a very long trip."

I notice that, on the days it is warm enough to take our journals outside, these older children have more stamina, write down more observations, and label their drawings without prompting. One day in March a young naturalist writes:

1. Signs of Spring—I found a small stream that went into the main stream and there were TONS of little green sprouts. A big sign of spring.

2. Laurie and I, with Joey, found worms and insects.

3. I almost caught a salamander! That's very rare at this time.

4. Laurie and I found a maple (?) with yellow water dripping from it. I thought it was very liquedy sap.

5. Laurie found this moss. It is called rough-stalked feather moss. (Written beneath a labeled drawing)

Another turns to poetry in mid-November:

Gray Winter
Softly falling like a
quiet blanket
as gray as a
dove, as soft as a feather
as cold as ice
sweep me in strong
winds, cool my anger,
and laughter drifts out
to match your cold.

As I did in June at the end of each school year, I ask my after-school students to reflect on their experiences at the stream on our last day:

I signed up for stream studies because I wanted to . . . see my old teacher again, go on more stream studies, and have fun. I recognized lots of creatures and learned the difference between the red back salamander and two line salamander. I also met a new friend in the natural world. This is called the puffball mushroom. I have really enjoyed the last four classes.

Victoria (fourth grade)

I signed up because it was the best time I had in second grade. I made a new friend, the camel cricket. I enjoyed this class, and I know I'm satis-fied that the camp is coming to an end. I hope to find a snake or two and at home I will continue being a big naturalist. I hope to sign up again, next year. I will also remember the Northern two-lined salaman-der, puffball mushrooms and the stream.

Daniel (fourth grade)

Of course there are still a handful of outdoor enthusiasts who want to "play." They continue to build dams, get lost in pretend adventures, or simply dig for salamanders. Since I have always considered children's *work* to be *play*, I am not worried. I reaffirm the importance of connecting children to the natural world and pick up the phone to arrange a day in the woods with my newest students—my granddaughters.

Appendix A: Second-Grade Narratives

FINDING A SPIDER

On Wednesday in stream study I was turning over rocks. I turned over one and then another and one more. I didn't see it at first but then I saw the spider.

I was happy. I had fun observing it. Me and Ariella noticed its poop is white and goopy. My mom noticed that all of the legs came out of the first section. A spider is made up of two parts; one is smaller than the other. We wondered what kind of spider it was and what it ate.

But then a fire drill happened. I didn't want to leave but I knew I had to go. I really didn't want to leave the spider. I could not wait until next Wednesday.

SHANNON (SEPTEMBER)

A HOLLOW LOG

It was stream study and Will was next to me and I was trying to study a hollow log. But the more I tried to study it the harder it got.

So I went closer. I wondered how long it was and how tall it would be if it was standing up like what it was like before it fell down. I also saw a piece of the inside of the tree. Will said, "Maybe we should put it together," but I just nod my eyes. After I estimated 100 inches, I wrote down my question.

After that Laurie said we could explore the natural world. I could walk across the log without falling. Will said, "Wow, how can you do that?" "Easy," I said. "Wow," said Will.

ERIN (SEPTEMBER)

THE TREE EXPERT

Once someone from Cornell came in. He was an expert on trees. First we stayed inside and studied the leaves we got the last stream study. I think mine is an Eastern white oak. Then it was our turn to go out. He showed us a hickory and its leaf. Then he told us that the bark of a hickory has huge ditches in its bark. Then he asked us which leaf we had and he told us a leaf I found, once again, was an Eastern oak. Then we did something fun. We wrapped our arms around to see how much people it took. As we were walking out of the woods, before we reached the end of the woods, he asked us what we learnt.

CHARLOTTE (OCTOBER)

HIKING AT BUTTERMILK FALLS

I was hiking at Buttermilk Falls. When we were halfway up the hill my feet were sore. When we were almost at the top I found a beautiful leaf. I didn't know what tree the leaf came from. I looked at it closely. I wondered if it was a cherry or ash leaf. Luckily I brang a leaf book. I checked the leaf book. I didn't find that leaf. I said, "Mom, I don't know what leaf this is."

IVY (OCTOBER)

THE TROUT TANK

One day at school, I walked in the class for the ordinary school morning stuff when I noticed some of my classmates looking at something. It was a tank, a fish tank! It was for the trout eggs that Laurie told us about! Though it was not on.

The next morning was pretty much the same except the fish tank was on! And the glass on the tank was foggy! After all the usual stuff we do in the morning, Laurie told us how the tank works and the day went on.

The next day we found the tank on again but the glass was no longer foggy! After we did our morning stuff Laurie read us a book about water. Aurora thought when the water got warm it evaporates. She was right.

LAURA (OCTOBER)

BLUE JAY

Once it was a misty day. There were some clouds and a little bit of sun. Suddenly I lifted my head up from reading 'cause I saw something blue move. I saw a blue jay at the bird feeder at school. We can see the bird feeder through the window. I examined the blue jay carefully. I noticed it had a black necklace. The blue jay had black under its tail. It had a black beak and eye. The blue jay flew over to a tree . . .

SOPHIE (FEBRUARY)

A SURPRISE AT THE WINDOW

We were reading when all of a sudden Theo said he saw a new bird. We all rushed to the window. People said it was an Ivory-billed woodpecker. Laurie said it was a pileated woodpecker. It was. We watched it peck the wood of a dead tree with chunks of wood falling to the ground. We also looked at the features.

Laurie went to get the camera. She tried to take a picture but when she tried to, it flew away. After that we wrote all our observations down in our journals and drew pictures. We used all our reading time, writing and drawing about the pileated woodpecker.

As soon as I got home, I raced into the house. "MOM, DAD, guess what we saw at school today?" I said out of breath. "A pileated woodpecker." After I told them, I sat right down and wrote a whole page about it.

LILY (FEBRUARY)

SURPRISE ON A DEAD TREE

One day in January we were reading a story called Rosa. Then Theo said Look! A new bird was on a dead tree. Everybody shouted "Pileated Woodpecker!" We saw the pileated woodpecker working its way up the tree. Laurie was so excited. She was going to go and get the camera. Then she came back. With one big pump of the bird's wings, it glided to Edward's house. Soon after, we talked about the features. Reading time was over. We spent our whole reading time on birds. It was time to go to music.

CHARLOTTE (FEBRUARY)

THE NEST

"Oh look, I think I saw a bird making a nest." Then I noticed my mom was talking. "Are you listening Rachel?" Then she pulled into a parking space and we walked into the restaurant.

I picked a table near a window. Then I looked out. I saw the same bird. It was pecking at the ground making a shallow hole. The bird pulled out some of its feathers and put it in the hole. Then it flew off. Then in a couple minutes it came back. Then my mom came with some food. "Mom," I said, "I think I see a bird making a nest!" My mom looked over through the window. "Oh I see the bird. Michael, James, come over here." They ran over. "What?" they asked. "Look out the window," I said. "There is a bird making a nest." They crawled across the seats and looked out the window. "How do you know *he*?" my brother said. I stopped him. "She," I said. "Whatever, how do you know she is making a nest?"

"Because I know birds put feathers on their nest to soften it up for their egg," I said. "Better eat your food now," said mom.

RACHEL (MAY)

THE HERO

At three o'clock I went outside to play lacrosse. I grabbed my stick, ball and my goal. I went to my back yard but I stood there like a pole stuck in the ground. I looked all around. I heard a noise. It went like this: ch ch ch ch ch ch ch ch ch. I ran so fast you would blink an eye and I would be back with binoculars. I looked all around. I saw some orange on a moving thing.

I ran back to my house and got a field guide of birds. And I ran back to my back yard. I found the bird again. It had a black head and it was very beautiful. I looked in the field guide. I looked up "oriole." It was on page 165. It was a . . . Baltimore oriole. I couldn't believe my ears and eyes. I had a smile from my hair to my hair. I fell down backwards. I told my family and they went to the back yard and fell down backwards too. I found a Baltimore oriole. I was the hero.

KEVIN (MAY)

THE GIANT MOTH

I was at Josh's going away party. It was at Fred's house. It was a sunny day and I was very hot. It was Sunday.

I was playing in the yard when I saw Fred's cat chasing a thing. To me it looked like a reptile. I called Fred and he said it was a giant mutated moth. "A moth?" I yelled. It seemed impossible. I could not believe that I was looking straight at a moth!

I showed my dad. He put it on a tree and we watched its wings come out.

ANDRES (MAY)

BUILDING A BIRD FEEDER

One Sunday my dad and I went to my grandfather's house. I liked going to my grandfather's house (who I called Poppie and my dad called Dad). I liked the birds that flew around outside. I liked the stuff he sold. And I liked the candy he kept in a jar. But the thing I liked about today is that we were going to build a bird feeder.

I got some wood. Poppie got a saw and I got some screws while my dad made lunch and we started. I held to a piece of wood while Poppie cut the wood so they would all be even. We kept doing it until lunch was ready. After lunch Poppie and I went outside to finish the bird feeder. I gave him screws and hit them in with a hammer.

Finally we were done. When it was time to go I gave Poppie a hug. I got in the van and I waved goodbye. I was happy to have a bird feeder.

FABIAN (MAY)

KINGFISHER

One really hot day Archy and his family were going to their friend's cabin. When they got to their friend's cabin, their two pet dogs barked and Pam and Julie came out of the cabin and they talked as the dogs settled down. Zip! "What's that?" Archy said.

It flew right . . . it flew left . . . but this time it flew like it was a shining blue brown and white skipping stone skipping on the water. It landed on a tree. "Wow!" said Archy. Shiny blue feathers and light white. It's a kingfisher. It flew into another tree and landed on a branch as it ate a minnow.

I felt really bouncy because I got to see a kingfisher skim across the water.

ALEX (MAY)

THE ROBIN'S NEST

It was a warm sunny day. I was talking to our garden helper Joseph, telling about the robin's nest Mama had discovered . . .

Then Mama called me over. She said, "Miryam, look at this." I hesitated. "At what?" I said. She sighed. I went over to her. There was bits of what looked like white eggshell. I felt sick. I turned one over. It was blue like the sky. In a flash I thought, "the robin's nest." An egg could of fallen out of the nest and shattered on the ground. I told Mama I thought an egg had fallen from the nest. Mama told me she thought the same thing. I shot over to her and squeezed her very tight now that it was time to show Joseph.

I raced over to Joseph, a piece of shell in my hand. I said, "Joseph, come look at this." I showed him the eggshell and while he went to look, I sat in the shadows and looked at the flowers in the flower garden. The sun shining on the petals seemed to remind me to let go of all worry. The robin would lay new eggs. I leaned forward to touch a petal. It was purple and silky.

MIRYAM (MAY)

CATCHING TADPOLES

It was a HOT spring day in May. Shannon was at Flat Rock. Shannon has light brown hair and hazel eyes that sparkle when she's happy. Shannon was looking at tadpoles in the water. Her sister, Mariah, was interested in mud. Her mother, Caitlin, was watching them.

Shannon wanted to catch a tadpole. Just in her hands. It was hard. Mud from the bottom kept rising up and hiding the tadpoles. She tried but whenever she got close to a tadpole it darted away. When she finally caught one it swam away quickly. She caught a few more but the same thing happened. She had to move to different places constantly because the water got too muddy. One time she caught one and it didn't swim away. She was delighted. She had become an expert on how to catch a tadpole.

Once she caught a shimmering tadpole. It was huge! She asked her mother to take a picture. Her mother did. The tadpole stayed there as if it liked it. Her sister wanted to hold a tadpole. Now she gave her the one she was holding. Shannon had a huge smile and her eyes were twinkling.

SHANNON (JUNE)

Appendix B: Second-Grade Poems

Heron

Lifts up its grand feet
And proudly walks through the clear water
Misty air
Rain falls through canopies
Of dark green leaves
Shaking the soggy morning air
Rain falls
On a heron's airy feathers
Mist grows
Around the wet foggy lagoon
Where a heron lives

—ANA

Downy Woodpecker in a Band

Downy
You are in a rock and roll band
You are the drummer
Thousands of other birds are cheering
Then you are selling T-shirts
Saying
"The Woodpeckers"

—ARJUN

Trees

Monsters
Outside the window
Traveling
Through the thick snow
Wind
Breaking
Branches

—RON

Snow

Snow, snow
When the sun
Beams
Down on you
It looks like a
Hundred
Shiny
Crystals
On the yard.

But when you
stick to the tree
your weight pulls
it down
and the tree
tumbles
to its fate.

—CHRISTIAN

Red Winged Blackbird

King of the world
Standing in the trees,
King of the world
Blowing in the breeze,
Black as coal,
And red as an apple,
White as a cloud,
It was a red winged blackbird
In its throne
Waiting to be served.

—ARJUN

The BOOMING
Of fire crackers
Bursts
The sky
Into spring
Yellow
Is daffodils
Green
Is the grass and trees
Blue
Is the trickle of water
Orange
Is the sun blaze
Brown
Is the buds on an oak tree
I love watching fire crackers
Burst
Into
Spring

—EVA

Whistling Wind

Hoooooooooooooo
Whistling wind
Soaring through the trees
Cracking branches on its way
Spitting air
Through its airy nostrils
Wind pulling grass toward it
With its strong arms
Lily flowers running
On the water
Being pushed by air and wind
Down river
To a world of unknown land

—ISABELLE

Leaves

Little ballerinas
Sailing through the sky
Twirling
Tossing
Rushing through the air
Soaring
Floating
Down through a blinding light
Shooting
Through feathery clouds
Dancing
On and on
Whirling
On and on
With the wind
Then finally floating down

—MIRYAM

Inside My Heart

Inside my heart,
Birds glide over the plains
Like waves lapping against the sand.
Inside my heart,
A flock of birds soars over the horizon
Like clouds racing over the sky.
Inside my heart,
Tree branches reach out to you
Like your mommy going to hug you.
A cardinal blaze of red
Like leaves falling in Autumn.
A robin blinding purple
Like a dying rose.

—STELLA

Trout Tank

You strain to look

As it darts

Left   Right

Up

Down

Like a torpedo
Through the water

Swish of tale
Flash of scale

Trout are fast

—JULIUS

Spring

When the flowers bloom,
The robins give a call,
Then you can be certain,
That snow won't fall.
Riding bikes
With only two wheels,
Doing something
Off your heels.
You see butterflies wing,
You hear birds sing,
You can also see
New green leaves twinkling.
Turkey vulture soars,
And thinks he's the best,
While he searches for sticks,
To make his nest.
Yes it's spring,
And now it's time
To ring the bluebells,
They go chime,
Chime!

—LAURA

Snowflakes

Snowflakes fall,
and sparkle together,
scatter themselves,
in the cold freezing weather.
Snowflakes shimmer,
snowflakes shine,
they'll fall anywhere,
on a house roof, a vine.
The snow piles high,
reaching for the
big,

                    blue,

                        northern

                            sky.

—LAURA

A Walk in Winter

Let us go
Let us go
Let us see the
Animals' prints in
The snow

Let us see
The water trickle
Down people's roof tops
And freeze into long
Winter's icicles

Let us see
The frosty gardens
On people's windows

Let us go
Let us go
On a sunny bright day of
winter

—LILY

The Peak

Far from the ground is
your point.

You sit there with
sun shining down on you.

I see you, sitting there
all alone.

Oh, wait there goes
a hawk.
Lands on your point.
He talks to you and you
talk to him.

You've made a new friend.

—SOPHIE

Appendix C: Recommended Websites

The following is a list of websites I most often used to enhance our study of the natural world. I include websites for students to use independently or with a partner, websites with identification tools for teachers, and sites with movies or other features suited to whole-class instruction.

When I chose a website for my students to use independently (those marked with an asterisk), I looked for authentic information and tried to avoid activities that turn out to be digital worksheets. With challenged readers in mind, I also looked for information that can be learned through photographs, videos, or sound recordings in addition to printed text.

I often turned to the Internet by myself when I was trying to identify a plant or animal encountered at our stream site. I list just a few of these identification sites to offer examples of user-friendly guides, but I suggest that you research similar ones best suited to your location.

Finally, I recommend sites with engaging videos to watch and discuss with your students.

BIRDS

The Cornell Lab of Ornithology All About Birds: Bird Guide
http://www.allaboutbirds.org/guide/search

With intuitive fingers, my students explore independently (and get lost in) this website. They search birds by name, shape, and image. Each bird can be explored through identification (text and photos), life history (text), sound, and video.

- -

The Feather Atlas: Flight Feathers of North American Birds
http://www.fws.gov/lab/featheratlas/idfeather.php

The U.S. Fish and Wildlife Service has created this tool for identifying the large flight feathers of a bird's wing and tail. Body feathers, which are usually soft, rounded, and with considerable "fluff" at the base are not included. It is particularly helpful for owl, hawk, and turkey feathers. I was thrilled, and surprised, when I was able to identify a mourning dove tail feather.

- -

INSECTS

Just for Kids: Let's Talk About Insects
http://urbanext.illinois.edu/kids/index.html

This is one of the pages developed by the University of Illinois Extension for its Urban Programs Resource Network. Each site on the Just for Kids menu presents information through pictures, text, and sound recording. The Let's Talk About Insects site uses cartoons and illustrations to provide an excellent review at the conclusion of an insect study.

- -

MIGRATION

Journey North: Weather and Songbird Migration
http://www.learner.org/jnorth/weather/AbornWeatherIndex.html

Whether you are studying birds, monarch butterflies, earthworms, frogs, whales, maple syrup production, or weather, you can track the movement and influence of weather patterns throughout the United States on color-coded maps. David Aborn of the North Chickamauga Creek Conservancy in Chattanooga, Tennessee, maintains this website and publishes weekly "Weather Forecasts for Migrating Songbirds" on Wednesdays from February through May. Click the Teachers link for additional slideshows or photo- and video-based observation activities that students can do themselves.

- -

PLANT IDENTIFICATION

Robert W. Freckmann Herbarium: Plants of Wisconsin
http://wisplants.uwsp.edu/Wisplants.html

You can search for wildflowers, trees, shrubs, vines, aquatic plants, ferns, and grasses using photographs or an "Identification Guide Questionnaire Form" that offers pictorial choices to narrow down the features of each plant. Once the plant is identified, there are links to Google searches for images and information. There are additional off-site links to identify fungi and lichens.

- -

STEWARDSHIP

Young Voices for the Planet

http://www.youngvoicesonclimatechange.com/

If you want to inspire your students to launch a stewardship project, check out this film series, created by Lynne Cherry—the author/illustrator of children's books such as The Great Kapok Tree, A River Ran Wild, *and others—and Gary Braash. Each short film (four to six minutes long) tells the story of young people who have successfully advocated for the environment and "reduced the carbon footprint of their homes, schools, and communities." For example, Olivia Bouler donated five hundred bird illustrations and raised $200,000 for Audubon's efforts to rescue birds after the BP Deepwater Horizon spill.*

Wangari Maathai: The Hummingbird

http://www.youtube.com/watch?v=fHtFM1XEXas&feature=related

This short video clip (2:24) features Wangari Maathai, a Nobel Peace Prize winner and the founder of the Green Belt Movement, an environmental organization in Kenya focused on the planting of trees, environmental conservation, and women's rights. She tells the Japanese story of a courageous hummingbird to deliver a simple and inspiring message: collectively we can make a difference.

TREE IDENTIFICATION

*Keys to Leaves of Virginia Trees

http://dendro.cnre.vt.edu/forsite/key/intro.htm

Jeff Kirwan, a Virginia Tech forestry professor and 4-H extension specialist, designed this web page for a Virginia 4-H tree identification project. With the mystery leaf close at hand, the viewer is led through a series of choices by clicking on the appropriate statement or image until a specific tree is determined: broad or needle-like leaves; alternate or opposite leaves; simple or compound leaves; lobes or no lobes; toothed or smooth edges.

WOODLAND HABITAT
Woods Walk
http://urbanext.illinois.edu/kids/index.html

This is another menu choice on Just for Kids, the University of Illinois Extension website listed earlier. It uses photographs to examine bark, fungi, lichen, moss, decomposition, plants, wildlife, and the natural hazards (poison ivy, ticks, etc.) found in a forest. There is also a place for students to make a journal entry or write a story and publish it on this website. The Teacher's Guide suggests recommended grade levels for each activity.

----

*Appropriate for independent student use, grade two and up.

References

Accorsi, William. 1993. *Rachel Carson*. New York: Holiday House.

Arnosky, Jim. 1992. *Crinkleroot's Guide to Knowing the Trees*. New York: Bradbury Press.

Art, Henry W., and Michael W. Robins. *Woods Walk*. North Adams, MA: Storey.

Avi. 1999. *Poppy and Rye*. New York: HarperCollins Children's Books.

_____. 2001. *Ereth's Birthday*. New York: HarperCollins Children's Books.

_____. 2005. *Poppy*. New York: HarperCollins Children's Books.

Baylor, Byrd. 1974. *Everybody Needs a Rock*. New York: Aladdin Books.

_____. 1997. *The Other Way to Listen*. New York: Aladdin Books.

Biddulph, Fred, and Jeanne Biddulph. 1993. *How Birds Live*. Sunshine Reader Series. St. Petersburg, FL: Wright Group.

Burton, Virginia Lee. 1969. *The Little House*. New York: Houghton Mifflin.

Calkins, Lucy. 2003. *Units of Study for Primary Writing*. Portsmouth, NH: Heinemann.

Cherry, Lynne. 1992. *A River Ran Wild*. San Diego, CA: Harcourt Brace.

_____. 1997. *Flute's Journey*. New York: Scholastic.

Demi. 2001. *Gandhi*. New York: Margaret K. McElderry Books.

Florian, Douglas. 1999. *Winter Eyes*. New York: Greenwillow Books.

FOSS/Lawrence Hall of Science. 2003. Air and Weather. Insects. FOSS Project Science Curriculums. Berkeley: University of California.

Fox, Mem. 1992. *Wilfred Gordon McDonald Partridge*. London: Puffin Books.

Gardner, Howard. 1983. *Frames of Mind: The Theory of Multiple Intelligences*. New York: Basic Books.

George, Kristine O'Connell. 1998. *Old Elm Speaks: Tree Poems*. New York: Clarion Books.

George, Lindsay Barrett. 1998. *In the Woods: Who's Been Here?* New York: Greenwillow Books.

Hammerstrom, Frances. 1975. *Walk When the Moon Is Full*. Freedom, CA: The Crossing Press.

Harrison, Hal H. 1975. *A Field Guide to Eastern Birds' Nests: United States East of the Mississippi River*. Boston: Houghton Mifflin.

Hines, Anna Grossnickle. 2001. *Pieces: A Year in Poems and Quilts*. New York: Greenwillow Books.

Keene, Ellin Oliver, and Susan Zimmerman. 2007. *Mosaic of Thought*. 2nd ed. Portsmouth, NH: Heinemann.

LaMarche, Jim. 2002. *The Raft*. New York: HarperCollins.

Lasky, Kathryn, and David Catrow. 1997. *She's Wearing a Dead Bird on Her Head*. New York: Disney-Hyperion.

Locker, Thomas. 1984. *Where the River Begins*. New York: Puffin Books.

Louv, Richard. 2005. *Last Child in the Woods: Saving Our Children from Nature-Deficit Disorder*. Chapel Hill, NC: Algonquin.

Lowry, Lois. 2009. *Crow Call*. New York: Scholastic.

Mazer, Anne. 1991. *The Salamander Room*. New York: Dragonfly.

McCullough, David. 2003. "The Title Always Comes Last." Jefferson Lecturer. Interview with NEH Chairman Bruce Cole. http://www.neh.gov/about/awards/jefferson-lecture/david-mccullough-interview.

Moskin, Marietta. 1978. *The Day of the Blizzard*. New York: Putnam Juvenile.

Peterson, Roger Tory. 1986. *Peterson First Guides: Birds; The Concise Field Guide to 188 Common Birds of North America*. New York: Houghton Mifflin.

Pilkey, Dav. 1999. *The Paperboy*. New York: Scholastic.

Pryor, Bonnie, and Beth Peck. 1992. *The House on Maple Street*. New York: Mulberry Books.

Robinson, Fay. 1995. *Where Do Puddles Go?* Rookie Read-About Science Series. New York: Children's Press.

Royston, Angela. 2003. *Life Cycle of an Oak Tree*. Chicago: Heinemann Library.

Rylant, Cynthia. 1995. *Gooseberry Park*. Orlando, FL: Harcourt.

_____. 1999. *Poppleton in Spring*. New York: Scholastic.

Sanders, Scott Russell. 1997. *Meeting Trees*. Washington, DC: National Geographic.

_____. 2002. *Crawdad Creek*. Washington, DC: National Geographic.

Schaffer, Donna. 2000. *Silkworms*. Life Cycles Series. Mankato, MN: Bridgestone Books.

Selsam, Millicent E. 1995. *How to Be a Nature Detective*. New York: HarperCollins.

Stevens, Carla. 1998. *Anna, Grandpa, and the Big Storm*. New York: Puffin Books.

Stokes, Donald, and Lillian Stokes. 1996. *Stokes Beginner's Guide to Birds: Eastern Region*. Stokes Field Guide Series. New York: Little, Brown.

Walsh, Ellen Stoll. 2002. *Dot & Jabber and the Mystery of the Missing Stream*. San Diego, CA: Harcourt.

Wetterer, Margaret K., and Charles M. Wetterer. 1996. *The Snow Walker*. Minneapolis, MN: Lerner.

Yolen, Jane. 2002. *Raising Yoder's Barn*. New York: Little, Brown.